Cambridge Elements

Elements in Epistemology
edited by
Stephen Hetherington
University of New South Wales, Sydney

ON BELIEVING AND BEING CONVINCED

Paul Silva Jr
University of Cologne

CAMBRIDGE
UNIVERSITY PRESS

Shaftesbury Road, Cambridge CB2 8EA, United Kingdom

One Liberty Plaza, 20th Floor, New York, NY 10006, USA

477 Williamstown Road, Port Melbourne, VIC 3207, Australia

314–321, 3rd Floor, Plot 3, Splendor Forum, Jasola District Centre, New Delhi – 110025, India

103 Penang Road, #05–06/07, Visioncrest Commercial, Singapore 238467

Cambridge University Press is part of Cambridge University Press & Assessment, a department of the University of Cambridge.

We share the University's mission to contribute to society through the pursuit of education, learning and research at the highest international levels of excellence.

www.cambridge.org
Information on this title: www.cambridge.org/9781009524148

DOI: 10.1017/9781009524117

When citing this work, please include a reference to the DOI: 10.1017/9781009524117

First published 2025

A catalogue record for this publication is available from the British Library

ISBN 978-1-009-52414-8 Hardback
ISBN 978-1-009-52415-5 Paperback
ISSN 2398-0567 (online)
ISSN 2514-3832 (print)

Additional resources for this publication at www.cambridge.org/Silva Jr

On Believing and Being Convinced

Elements in Epistemology

DOI: 10.1017/9781009524117
First published online: January 2025

Paul Silva Jr
University of Cologne

Author for correspondence: Paul Silva Jr, psilvajr@gmail.com

Abstract: Our doxastic states are our belief-like states, and these include *outright* doxastic states and *degreed* doxastic states. The former include believing that *p*, having the opinion that *p*, thinking that *p*, being sure that *p*, being certain that *p*, and doubting that *p*. The latter include degrees of confidence, credences, and perhaps some phenomenal states. But we also have *conviction* (being convinced *simpliciter* that *p*) and *degrees of conviction* (being *more or less* convinced that *p*). This Element shows: how and why *all* of the outright doxastic states mentioned above can be reduced to conviction thresholds; what degrees of conviction fundamentally are (degreed reliance-dispositions); why degrees of conviction are not credences; when suspending a belief is compatible with continuing to believe; and the surprising extent to which Kant endorsed the theory of conviction that emerges in this Element.

Keywords: belief, convinced, conviction, credence, certainty, confidence

ISBNs: 9781009524148 (HB), 9781009524155 (PB), 9781009524117 (OC)
ISSNs: 2398-0567 (online), 2514-3832 (print)

Contents

1 Introduction 1

2 Conviction and Its Doxastic Neighbourhood 2

3 Degrees of Conviction and the Reduction of Outright States 16

4 The Metaphysics of Belief and Degrees of Conviction 21

5 The *Sui Generity* of Degrees of Conviction 33

6 Belief-Suspension Compatibilism 40

7 Was Kant a Kantian about Doxastic States? by Christopher Benzenberg 51

References 62

1 Introduction

The study of belief and its norms of rationality is a central part of contemporary epistemology. But belief is just one of many doxastic states. When it comes to the class of doxastic states, epistemologists commonly distinguish between our *outright* doxastic states and our *degreed* doxastic states. The outright doxastic states include believing that *p*, thinking that *p*, having the opinion that *p*, being sure that *p*, being certain that *p*, and doubting that *p*. Our degreed doxastic states include degrees of confidence, credences, and certain degreed phenomenal states.

However, in addition to the outright doxastic states mentioned above we also have **conviction**, that is, the state of being convinced (*simpliciter*) that something is the case. And in addition to the degreed states mentioned in the previous paragraph we have **degrees of conviction**, that is, being *more or less* convinced that something is the case. The concept of conviction was central to Kant's way of thinking about our doxastic states. However, conviction has not been regarded as a distinctive doxastic mental state in recent philosophy of mind and epistemology. The aim of this Element is to locate and defend the distinctive place of conviction and its degrees among our doxastic states.

When it comes to our doxastic states there are two kinds of questions we can ask. We can ask questions about their nature:

> **Nature Question**. For any agent *S* and doxastic state *D*, what is it for *S* to be in state *D*?

But we can also ask questions about their structure:

> **Structural Question**. For any doxastic states *D1 . . . Dn*, how are *D1 . . . Dn* related to each other?

Section 2 begins with a suggestive Kantian answer to the Structural Question. It then provides evidence for a version of a Kantian picture on which we have at least three outright doxastic states, where thinking is the logically weakest state, certainty is the logically strongest state, and conviction stands between them. A version of Foley's (1992) reductive Lockean approach to our outright doxastic states is considered. On this view, we can account for all our outright doxastic states in terms of *confidence thresholds*. This view is rejected, owing to the psychological possibility of having a very high degree of confidence in *p* while failing to believe, or think, or be convinced that *p*.

Section 3 provides an alternative view. It demonstrates the foundations for thinking that conviction comes in degrees and shows how degrees of conviction provide what is needed for a distinctive Kantian Threshold View of our outright doxastic states. For some readers, the Kantian Threshold View will not appear very different from its Lockean counterpart. This is likely owed to the following presupposition:

> **Conviction–Confidence Identity**. Degrees of conviction just are degrees of confidence.

But this presupposition is plagued with problems. However, to appreciate these problems we first need to answer the Nature Question in regard to degrees of conviction. Section 4 does this, arguing that one's degree of conviction in *p* is, roughly, the strength of one's disposition to rely on *p*.

Section 5 defends the *sui generity* of degrees of conviction. In particular, this section explains how and why degrees of conviction separate from degrees of confidence (credences) and other degreed doxastic states, including felt degrees of confidence, the feeling of conviction, and degrees of revisability. It also provides an ecumenical suggestion about how best to understand talk of 'degrees of belief'.

Section 6 uses facts about masking dispositions to explain how and why we can *simultaneously* believe (/think, /be convinced, /be certain) that *p* while also suspending these very states. This is a significant result as it's usually assumed that suspending an attitude necessarily involves *lacking* that attitude; that is, believing that *p* and suspending belief that *p* are incompatible. This incompatibilist idea is central to many epistemic problems and has been used to motivate dilemmas of rationality. But if belief and the suspension of belief are compatible states, then once-paradoxical cases arguably cease to be paradoxical.

Section 7 turns to historical questions about the extent to which Kant was himself a 'Kantian' in our sense. It turns out that Kant's theory of doxastic states was surprisingly Kantian as he prominently discusses conviction *simpliciter* and occasionally comments on degrees of conviction. Further, there is some evidence that Kant thought about states such as opinion and certainty in terms of degrees of conviction. Lastly, Kant's concept of degrees of conviction is open to (or at least not in tension with) the dispositional analysis of degrees of conviction.

2 Conviction and Its Doxastic Neighbourhood

Belief is the paradigmatic outright doxastic state, and many studies of our outright doxastic states start with belief. This study is different. It begins with a summary of Kant's views about the outright doxastic states, which motivates an exploration of a body of linguistic evidence for the idea that we have at least three distinct outright doxastic states that involve taking a positive stance towards a proposition: thinking, conviction, and certainty. Reflection on Kant's theory of assent motivates the idea that these are strength-ordered in the following way: thinking is the logically weakest state (entailing none of the others), certainty the logically strongest state (entailing all of the others), and conviction stands between (entailing only itself and thinking). We explain why a Lockean Threshold View cannot account for these structural facts, and in the following section we introduce a Kantian Threshold View.

2.1 A Kantian Approach to the Doxastic Attitudes

This section quickly introduces one interpretation of Kant's understanding of our fundamental doxastic states that stands out to us for the simple reason that it provides the starting point for a promising way of approaching the nature of the outright doxastic states and their relation to degreed doxastic states in philosophy of mind and epistemology.

When it comes to our doxastic states Kant introduces a central and organizing doxastic concept that he calls *Fürwahrhalten*, which literally means 'holding to be true', but is more commonly translated as 'assent'. **Assent**, as a genus, should be thought of as a purely doxastic state and one that sits atop a gothic taxonomy with many species and subspecies that are individuated by various further characteristics (A820–31/B848–59).[1] To begin to get a grip on this taxonomy, consider any arbitrary case in which an agent assents to *p*. Kant suggests that of any case of assent we can ask at least the following questions:

> **Normative Questions**. Is the agent's state of assent justified by the agent's grounds/reasons to any degree? If so, is there a *sufficient* degree of justification for being in that state? Is the justification in question provided by evidential and/or non-evidential grounds/reasons?[2]
>
> **Voluntaristic Questions**. Did the agent come to assent to *p* just by choosing to do so? That is, is the agent's state of assent within their direct voluntary control?[3]

[1] German translations of English sentences are due to the collective effort of the 2023 CONCEPT research group at the University of Cologne, with Chris Benzenberg and Lena Ghareh Baghery shouldering most of the load. The historical scholarship contained in this volume and the translations of Kant are due to Chris Benzenberg. We cite the *Critique of Pure Reason* by the A edition (1781) and B edition (1787). Other references to Kant are to the volume and page of the Academy edition. Reflections are also cited by their R number. For reconstructions of Kant's taxonomy of assent, see Stevenson (2003), Chignell (2007a,2007b), and Pasternack (2014).

[2] Kant's terms for evidential/non-evidential justification are 'objective grounds' and 'subjective/practical grounds'. Whether *S*'s grounds are objective or subjective depends, in part, on whether the grounds for *S*'s assent are universally valid or only valid for *S* (A820–1/B848–9; 24:150).

[3] For Kant, an answer to this question can be implied by an answer to the previous question because a state of assent is within one's direct voluntary control just in case it doesn't rest on sufficient

Doxastic Question. How strong is the agent's state of assent? That is, *how strongly* does the agent take *p* to be true?

Kant derives different species of assent based on how these questions get answered. For example, knowledge (*Wissen*) is a species of assent for Kant that requires assenting to *p* in response to sufficient evidential grounds, where these grounds force one to assent to *p* and thus put one's assent outside of one's direct voluntary control.[4] And knowledge, for Kant, additionally involves the strongest degree of assent. Faith (*Glaube*) is another species of assent for Kant, which requires assenting to *p* on sufficient non-evidential, practical grounds. Unlike knowledge, faith is within one's direct voluntary control. But, like knowledge, faith for Kant requires the strongest degree of assent.[5]

However, while most species of assent respond to all three questions, Kant occasionally also identifies instances of assent that *only* respond to the Doxastic Question. These species of assent involve purely doxastic attitudes that can be characterized by differences in their strength. Put differently, Kant seems to have recognized that agents can assent more or less strongly, and that this feature of a state of assent can be described independently of its normative and voluntaristic features. These doxastic states have been largely ignored in the recent literature on Kant's theory of assent, mainly because they don't feature prominently in the standard taxonomy. Yet they are the ones we'll be focusing on.

Kant identified three kinds of assent in relation to how strong one's state of assent could be. First among these is **certainty (*Gewissheit*)** or more precisely what Kant calls 'subjective certainty' (24:437). Subjective certainty arguably aligns with what we now call 'psychological certainty' and indicates the strongest state of assent.[6] Next is Kant's notion of **conviction (*Überzeugung*)**, specifically his notion of 'subjective conviction' (A824/B852). This consists of

objective grounds (Benzenberg forthcoming). Since the voluntarist profile of assent aligns with its normative profile for Kant, it cannot be used to derive new species of assent that we could not have already derived via the normative profile.

4 See (A822/B850), (R2507, 16:397–8), (24:158), among many other passages.

5 See especially (A823–9/B851–7), (5:472), and (R2462, 16:380).

6 See (R2450, 16:373), (R2459, 16:378), and (R5645, 18:291). This psychological sense of 'subjective certainty' is not to be confused with a normative sense of the same term. Kant sometimes also uses 'subjective certainty' to denote the practical-moral certainty of faith (R6099, 18:452). Moral certainty results from sufficient subjective grounds, which in the case of faith, point to a special kind of subjective-practical *justification* (A823/B851). Note also that for Kant, not all certainty is subjective certainty; Kant's notion of 'logical certainty', for example, roughly corresponds to what many today call 'epistemic certainty' (A822/B850; A829/B857). More on this in Section 7.1.

a strong – Kant uses the term 'firm' (A824/B852) – state of assent. Weaker than both of them is **opinion (*Meinung*)**. Opinion is a bit tricky because Kant also defines it with reference to the Normative Question and its degree of evidential support (A822/B850). But insofar as the strength of opinion is proportional to its evidence,[7] we can bracket this normative dimension and focus entirely on opinion as a weak state of assent, which one might call 'subjective opinion' to keep with Kant's naming scheme. On Kant's account, there is no weaker state of assent than subjective opinion.[8] Since what follows is just about our doxastic states, we will drop the 'subjective' qualifier. Putting a picture to these strength-ordered states of assent, we have Figure 1.

There is much more to say about this interpretation of Kant's theory of assent and its relation to contemporary ways of thinking about our doxastic states. We'll return to this in Section 7. For now these quick remarks on Kant inspire new ways of approaching the structural relations that obtain among our doxastic states. First of all, it is somewhat uncommon for epistemologists to theorize about opinion, but opinions are among our doxastic states. Second, it is especially uncommon for epistemologists to theorize about conviction, that is, the state of being convinced. But it too is among our doxastic states. Third, it is somewhat uncommon to seek to organize our outright doxastic states as standing in something like a genus–species relation (or, at the very least, a generality relation), where the most general outright state entailed by all the other more specific states involves the idea of 'holding a proposition as true'. But in what follows we will argue that this broadly Kantian picture of our outright doxastic states is correct.

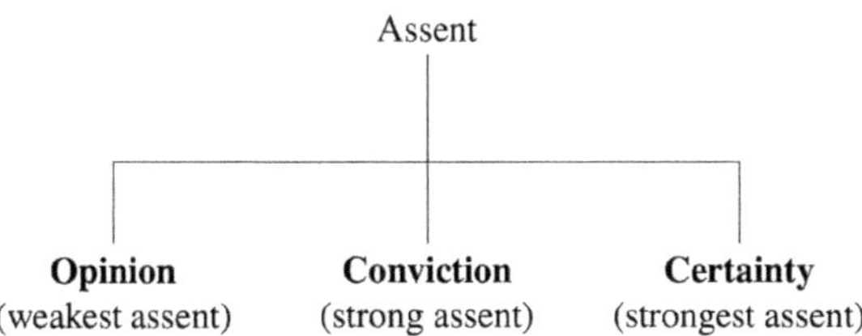

Figure 1 Taxonomy of strength-ordered assent.

[7] See Kant's discussion in the *Logic Blomberg* (24:219). See also Willaschek (2010:189), Pasternack (2011:291,2014:45), and Gava (2019:56–7).

[8] Kant sets the same lower threshold for opinion as he does for assent (24:144; 24:825). Only once, in the third *Critique*, does Kant suggest that there is assent weaker than opinion, namely hypothesis (5:463). But this passage is an outlier that can safely be ignored; after all, Kant typically classifies hypothesis as a species of opinion (24:733). In the same spirit, Chignell notes that Kant classifies 'hunches, working assumptions, and scientific hypotheses' simply as 'weakly-held opinions' (2007b:37). We agree with this reading.

2.2 Natural Language on Thinking, Conviction, and Certainty

Linguistic evidence supports the Kantian idea that our folk theory of mind references at least three distinct outright doxastic states that admit a strength-ordering involving opinion/thinking, conviction, and certainty. This idea runs contrary to an emerging line of thought that natural language (or at least English) makes no reference to any outright doxastic state that stands between thinking and certainty.[9] If correct, there is no outright doxastic state that stands between thinking and certainty in terms of strength.[10] But what has been overlooked is *conviction.* And it is not hard to see that conviction has a distinctive place in our economy of doxastic states.

To begin to see this, take the following expressions, which ascribe outright doxastic states to agents:

(1) *S* thinks that *p*. / It is *S*'s opinion that *p*.
(1′) *S denkt, dass p. / Es ist S' Meinung, dass p.*

(2) *S* is convinced that *p*.
(2′) *S ist (davon) überzeugt, dass p.*

(3) *S* is certain that *p*.
(3′) *S ist (sich) gewiss, dass p.*

Expressions (1)–(3′) are a familiar part of everyday thought and talk. The task to follow is to explore their relational features.

The first thing to highlight is that '*S* thinks that *p*' ('*S denkt, dass p*') and 'It is *S*'s opinion that *p*' ('*Es ist S' Meinung, dass p*') are expressions that seem to refer to the same doxastic state in both English and German. Consider separating them:

(4) ?He thinks that she arrived, but it's not his opinion that she arrived.
(4′) ?*Er denkt, dass sie angekommen ist, aber es ist nicht seine Meinung, dass sie angekommen ist.*

---

[9] See Hawthorne et al. (2016), Dorst (2019), Rothschild (2020), Holguín (2022), Goodman and Holguín (2023), and Goodman (2023).

[10] In response, some have insightfully argued that we can construct a semi-technical notion of 'strong/outright/full belief' that is stronger than 'believes'/'thinks' in English but also weaker than 'sure'/'certainty' in English. For example, Schulz (2021a) argues that we should theorize with 'outright belief' stipulatively defined as the strongest belief state implied by knowledge. This clever approach has noteworthy limitations. First, there is evidence for weak knowledge; this is implied by Turri's (2015,2016) defence of unreliable knowledge. Second, this stipulative approach leaves open questions about the total class of our outright doxastic states that we seem to refer to with natural language and how they are related to degreed states we seem to refer to. Lastly, there are independent criticisms of semi-technical ways of constructing a concept of 'strong/outright/full belief' in the way that Schulz and others do. See Goodman's (2023) 'The Myth of Full Belief'. See also Heil (2021:ch.4) for a related discussion of Schulz.

(5) ?It's his opinion that she arrived, but he does not think that she arrived.
(5′) ?*Es ist seine Meinung, dass sie angekommen ist, aber er denkt nicht, dass sie angekommen ist.*

These strike us as not only odd-sounding, but also as semantically infelicitous. Should that be so, we will have strong evidence for the following identity:

T=O Necessarily, *S* thinks that *p* iff it is *S*'s opinion that *p*.
Notwendigerweise gilt, S denkt, dass p, genau dann, wenn es S' Meinung ist, dass p.

But not all are happy with T=O. Some informants report that 'It's her opinion that *p*' carries information about the weakness of one's evidential position in regard to *p*. We think this is a pragmatic implicature where the term 'just' is typically heard implicitly and is taken to convey something about the weakness of one's evidential position, as in 'It's *just* her opinion that *p*'. This implicature can also be provoked by adding 'just' to thinking claims, as in 'She *just* thinks that *p*'. Arguably, hearing the silent 'just' is a result of an expectation that speakers conform to the Gricean maxim of quantity: be as informative as one can, and give just as much information as is needed for current conversational aims. For, typically, if one is as informative as is relevant and one is convinced/certain that *p*, one will not indicate only that it's one's opinion that *p*. Further, the sense of evidential weakness associated with opinion comes from the expectation that rational agents proportion their doxastic attitudes to their evidence. Thus, if one just has the opinion (/just thinks) that *p*, this would suggest that one's evidence isn't strong enough for being convinced or certain.[11] We emphasize: nothing turns on T=O in Sections 2, 3, 4, 5, and 6. So we'll sidestep the issue of T=O by privileging 'thinks that' in what follows. We leave it to those who disagree with T=O to say what opinion is and how it differs from thinking-that.

When it comes to discussions of certainty it is standard to distinguish epistemic certainty from psychological certainty, where 'psychological certainty' refers to whatever doxastic state is implicated by the expression '*S* is certain that *p*'. In contrast, 'epistemic certainty' is widely used to refer to whatever condition the expression 'It is certain that *p*' refers to. In what follows we are only concerned with psychological certainty.

It is clearly possible to think that something is true while not being certain that it is. We think a friend will visit today because they said so. But we aren't certain that they will since transportation strikes are not unusual in Cologne. Thus, we have:

[11] In relation to the fact that certainty entails thinking/opinion on our view, one informant noted that they would never say 'It's my opinion that my name is . . . ', but it's something they would say they are certain of. This is also explainable by a Gricean maxim of quantity.

T1 It is possible that *S* thinks that *p*, but *S* is not certain that *p*.
Es ist möglich, dass S denkt, dass p, aber S (sich) nicht gewiss ist, dass p.

Additionally, we may observe that certainty entails thinking. That is:

T2 Necessarily, if *S* is certain that *p*, then *S* thinks that *p*.
Notwendigerweise gilt, wenn S (sich) gewiss ist, dass p, dann denkt S, dass p.

Were T2 false, statements like the following should sound fine:

(6) #I'm certain that he arrived, but I don't think that he arrived.
(6′) *#Ich bin (mir) gewiss, dass er angekommen ist, aber ich denke nicht, dass er angekommen ist.*

(7) #She's certain that he arrived, but she doesn't think that he arrived.
(7′) *#Sie ist (sich) gewiss, dass er angekommen ist, aber sie denkt nicht, dass er angekommen ist.*

But they sound far from fine, and T2 explains their infelicity.

Let's bridge **conviction** and thinking. By 'conviction' we always mean to be referring to *the state of being convinced*. This is not unnatural. For when the noun 'conviction' is used with a sentential complement – 'conviction that' – it tends to be used to refer to the same state that the adjectival expression 'convinced that' does. Some dictionaries inter-define these expressions.[12] It does not matter for the present purposes whether the noun phrase 'conviction that' has other uses in natural language that refer to some other kind of doxastic state. For we will always work with the adjectival expression 'convinced that' and we use 'conviction' as a convenient noun to refer to the state of being convinced.[13]

In regard to conviction and thinking, it is evident that conviction entails thinking:

T3 Necessarily, if *S* is convinced that *p*, then *S* thinks that *p*.
Notwendigerweise gilt, wenn S (davon) überzeugt ist, dass p, dann denkt S, dass p.

---

[12] For example, the on-line Merriam-Webster dictionary says that conviction is 'the state of being convinced'. www.merriam-webster.com/dictionary/conviction.

[13] We can test the potential equivalence of 'convinced that' and 'conviction that' by considering conjunctions like: 'It is *S*'s conviction that it's wrong to harm innocents, but *S* is not convinced that it's wrong to harm innocents.' This strikes us as odd. Similarly odd is the claim that '*S* is convinced that it's wrong to harm innocents, but it's not *S*'s conviction that it is wrong to harm innocents.' If there is a difference, perhaps it is because there are uses of 'conviction that' which seem to implicate not only being convinced, but also some degree of commitment to remaining so convinced or to somehow promoting that which one is convinced of. But it is not clear to us whether these are semantic implications or pragmatic implicatures.

As evidence for T3 consider claims like:

(8) #I am convinced that he arrived, but I don't think that he arrived.
(8′) *#Ich bin (davon) überzeugt, dass er angekommen ist, aber ich denke nicht, dass er angekommen ist.*

(9) #She is convinced that he arrived, but she doesn't think that he arrived.
(9′) *#Sie ist (davon) überzeugt, dass er angekommen ist, aber sie denkt nicht, dass er angekommen ist.*

These don't make sense. Plausibly, this is because conviction entails thinking.

The last entailment we wish to highlight is that certainty entails conviction:

T4 Necessarily, if *S* is certain that *p*, then *S* is convinced that *p*.
Notwendigerweise gilt, wenn S (sich) gewiss ist, dass p, dann ist S (davon) überzeugt, dass p.

Again, we find evidence for T4 by considering the oddity of instances that run contrary to it:

(10) #I am certain that he arrived, but I am not convinced that he arrived.
(10′) *#Ich bin (mir) gewiss, dass er angekommen ist, aber ich bin nicht (davon) überzeugt, dass er angekommen ist.*

(11) #She is certain that he arrived, but she is not convinced that he arrived.
(11′) *#Sie ist (sich) gewiss, dass er angekommen ist, aber sie ist nicht (davon) überzeugt, dass er angekommen ist.*

The readiest explanation for the contradictory sound of these is T4.

Thinking is not just logically weaker than conviction and certainty (in the sense that it entails neither); it seems normatively weaker (in the sense that it's less evidentially demanding). Let's illustrate this:

Track Race. Take a three-horse race. You know that horse A is more likely to win than horses B and C. You know the probability of A winning is 52%, and of B winning is 24%, and of C winning is 24%. When asked who you think will win, you answer: 'I think horse A will win' – all the while knowing that there is a very good chance that A will not win.[14]

Cases like Track Race are quite ordinary and quite easily constructed:

[14] This is a modification of a case in Hawthorne et al. (2016). I've moved the probability of A winning above 0.5.

Diagnosis. Dr House is treating a patient Sarah in New York with symptoms that are common to five different diseases: A–E. However, House knows that A is not uncommon in New York, but B–E are somewhat uncommon in New York – they are diseases that are usually contracted outside city environments and Sarah rarely travels outside the city. The probabilities of A–E are: Pr(A) = 0.52, Pr(B) = Pr(C) = Pr(D) = Pr(E) = 0.12. When asked to identify Sarah's disease, House answers: 'I think she has disease A.'[15]

Many have argued that one need not speak falsely nor need one manifest any irrationality when claiming that 'I think horse A will win' or 'I think she has disease A' so long as these outcomes are sufficiently more likely than all their competitor outcomes. Indeed, some think that the probability of the accepted outcome can be *less than 0.5*.[16] But here lies a controversy we need not engage. We will limit ourselves to the following lesson:

T5 There are at least some cases where it is rational for *S* to think that *p* even if *S* knows that: while *p* is more likely than ¬*p*, ¬*p* is almost as likely as *p*.
Es gibt zumindest einige Fälle, in denen es für S rational ist, zu denken, dass p, selbst wenn S weiß, dass p zwar wahrscheinlicher ist als ¬p, aber ¬p fast so wahrscheinlich ist wie p.

Cases like Track Race and Diagnosis not only provide evidence for the normative weakness of thinking, but also its *logical weakness* relative to conviction. For example, an agent in Track Race might well think that A will win without being convinced that A will win. It would not be incoherent or surprising to hear an agent say in such a case: 'I think that A will win, but I'm not convinced.' This suggests:

T6 It is possible that *S* thinks that *p*, but *S* is not convinced that *p*.
Es ist möglich, dass S denkt, dass p, aber S nicht (davon) überzeugt ist, dass p.

An additional piece of evidence for T6 stems from the phenomenon of *neg-raising* associated with weak mental state terms. When we say '*S* doesn't think that *p*' we tend to provoke the implicature that '*S* thinks that not-*p*'. For example, uses of 'You don't think that she's home' suggest that 'You

---

[15] Inspiration for this case is from Turri (2015,2016), where he argues for the possibility of unreliable knowledge in cases structurally akin to this. As in Track Race, I have moved the probability of A above 0.5.

[16] See Hawthorne et al. (2016), Dorst (2019), Rothschild (2020), Holguín (2022), and Goodman and Holguín (2023). This idea is noteworthy in the present context since, on Chignell's (2021) reading of Kant, Kant himself seemed to allow for something like 'improbable opinion' (119). See also Chignell (2007a:327,2007b:44) and Section 7.1.

think that she's not home'. In contrast, this doesn't occur with strong mental state terms like 'certain' and 'sure': stating that someone isn't certain that p does not suggest that they are certain that $\neg p$.[17] 'Convinced' functions like 'certain' in regard to neg-raising: uses of 'You're not convinced that she's home' does not suggest that 'You are convinced that she's not home'. If the neg-raising behaviour of 'thinks' and the absence of such behaviour with 'certain' is evidence that thinking can separate from certainty, then we have the same kind of evidence for the idea that thinking can separate from conviction.

While intuitions about the rationality of thinking in cases like Track Race and Diagnosis provide some evidence that thinking is normatively weak, they provide no evidence that conviction or certainty are normatively weak. We cannot, without introducing a significant degree of irrationality, add to Track Race that you are either convinced or certain that horse A will win:

(12) While the evidence ensures that A is more likely to win than to lose, it also ensures that A is almost as likely to lose. So I'm convinced (/certain) that A will win.

(12′) *Die Hinweise*[18] *stellen zwar sicher, dass A wahrscheinlicher gewinnt als verliert, aber sie stellen auch sicher, dass A fast genauso wahrscheinlich verliert. Ich bin also (davon) überzeugt (/(mir) gewiss), dass A gewinnen wird.*

These statements sound problematic. Not because they represent psychological impossibilities, but because they each involve a non-trivial measure of irrationality. This suggests:

T7 It is irrational for S to be convinced that p or certain that p if S knows that: while p is more likely than $\neg p$, $\neg p$ is almost as likely as p.
Es ist irrational für S, (davon) überzeugt zu sein, dass p oder (sich) gewiss zu sein, dass p, wenn S weiß, dass p zwar wahrscheinlicher ist als ¬p, aber ¬p fast so wahrscheinlich ist wie p.

Lastly, we note that conviction can separate from certainty:

T8 It is possible that S is convinced that p, but S is not certain that p.
Es ist möglich, dass S (davon) überzeugt ist, dass p, aber S (sich) nicht gewiss ist, dass p.

[17] See Hawthorne et al. (2016:1399) and Rothschild (2020:1348) for discussion.

[18] There are many German words that translate the English term 'evidence', such as *Evidenz*, *Beweis*, *Indiz*, *Anzeichen*, *Beleg*, *Nachweis*, *Befund*, and even *Spur*. They all have (slightly) different connotations and are used in different contexts. 'Hinweis' is a solid translation here.

Examples are not hard to provide here. I am convinced that the Phoenicians were skilled sailors because I seem to remember my Roman history professor, Gary Ferngren, asserting this. But reflecting on the fallibility of historical evidence for events long past and my very limited historical knowledge, I would also say that I'm not certain of this. Similarly, I'm now convinced that my bike has not been stolen from my apartment basement. But knowing that all kinds of people have access to my apartment basement I would not say that I'm certain of this.[19] In general, when we are inclined to explicitly note that our evidence for *p* is very strong and yet fallible in a way that is worth not completely ignoring, statements of the following form sound just fine:

(13) ✓I am convinced that *p*, but I am not certain that *p*.
(13′) ✓*Ich bin (davon) überzeugt, dass p, aber ich bin (mir) nicht gewiss, dass p.*

Let's now take stock. We've said nothing about belief. We'll get to that. About thinking, conviction, and certainty, the following set of claims are well supported:

T1 It is possible that *S* thinks that *p*, but *S* is not certain that *p*.
T2 Necessarily, if *S* is certain that *p*, then *S* thinks that *p*.
T3 Necessarily, if *S* is convinced that *p*, then *S* thinks that *p*.
T4 Necessarily, if *S* is certain that *p*, then *S* is convinced that *p*.
T5 There are at least some cases where it is rational for *S* to think that *p* even if *S* knows that: while *p* is more likely than $\neg p$, $\neg p$ is almost as likely as *p*.
T6 It is possible that *S* thinks that *p*, but *S* is not convinced that *p*.
T7 It is irrational for *S* to be convinced that *p* or certain that *p* if *S* knows that: while *p* is more likely than $\neg p$, $\neg p$ is almost as likely as *p*.
T8 It is possible that *S* is convinced that *p*, but *S* is not certain that *p*.

There are a few final issues to note before moving on. We've said little about *doubt*. Three options arise in the present context: treat doubt (*simpliciter*) as the contradictory of thinking, or of conviction, or of certainty. Perhaps, when it comes to propositions one has considered, one doubts that *p* just in case one is not convinced that *p*. Given the way in which thinking separates from

[19] Perhaps further evidence for T8 comes from the legal literature where fact finders are asked to assess whether the evidence is 'clear and convincing', where this standard of evidence is explicitly intended to leave room for a small degree of reasonable doubt. This suggests that evidence can warrant being convinced without warranting certainty. But that only makes sense if they are distinct states. See www.law.cornell.edu/wex/clear_and_convincing_evidence.

conviction, this leaves room for doubting that *p* while thinking that *p*. This can sound odd in the abstract, but it's less odd in the kinds of cases where thinking and conviction separate from each other, that is, Track Race and Diagnosis. However, we suspect some readers may prefer to treat doubt as the contradictory of thinking or certainty. This raises questions we cannot here consider, and nothing will turn on one's preferred account of doubt in what follows.[20]

The concept of *surety* is also among our outright doxastic concepts. But how is surety related to the other outright doxastic states? Goodman and Holguín (2023:640) have it that in English '*S* is sure that *p*' means the same as '*S* is certain that *p*'. Lassiter (2017:123) identifies a similarly tight semantic connection between 'sure' and 'certain'. If correct, then the place of surety just is the place of certainty. We find this connection between certainty and surety intuitive. We have additional questions about surety, but we set them aside,[21] for the semantic evidence for theorizing about conviction and degrees of conviction is reasonably clear and tractable. Further, by advancing our understanding of the relationships between believing, thinking, conviction, and certainty we will aid those seeking to advance our understanding of surety.

2.3 The Failure of the Lockean Threshold View

What could explain T1–T8? Foley (1992,1993) has defended a pair of influential 'Lockean' claims that can easily be extended to explain T1–T8. Here's that extension. Start with the widely shared idea that we have **degrees of confidence** in various claims. Next, identify each kind of outright doxastic state with different threshold-exceeding levels of confidence. For example, on the scale representing our degrees of confidence, let us just specify different thresholds: a thinking threshold that requires some non-trivial

[20] See Unger (1975) and Moon (2018).

[21] Here is something that troubles us about identifying surety with certainty. 'I'm convinced, but I wouldn't say I'm certain' sounds fine. But 'I'm convinced, but I wouldn't say I'm sure' sounds odd. *If* the latter is indeed semantically infelicitous, perhaps one way of explaining the attraction of treating 'sure' and 'certain' as synonyms while observing that 'sure' seems to have some connection to conviction in the absence of certainty, is to attribute to 'sure' a dynamic semantic function. One suggestion along these lines is that 'sure' picks out conviction rather than certainty only in contexts where (i) one is convinced but not certain, and (ii) the error possibilities left open by one's conversational context that make certainty inappropriate are not salient. So what makes 'I'm convinced, but I wouldn't say I'm sure' sound problematic is that stating the second conjunct somehow *makes* previously non-salient error possibilities salient. But when one properly ignores all error possibilities, then manifestations of conviction in such cases will look like manifestations of certainty. All of this raises more questions than we have space to address. Again, we think making headway on our understanding of the neglected status of conviction can help with future work, and that's the point of this Element.

degree of confidence, followed by a conviction threshold that requires a higher degree of confidence, and a certainty threshold to be identified with the highest level of confidence. Add to this the further normative thesis that one should proportion one's confidence level to one's evidence and you'll be able to derive T1–T8. Putting all of this into a picture we have Figure 2.

First, the hollow box on the left marks the zero-degree point on the scale, while the filled-in box marks the maximum. The exact placement of the thinking and conviction thresholds is not relevant for our purposes. So we use the squiggly segment in each line to indicate our silence on the geometrical distances, and thus to discourage readers from drawing inferences about the proportion of the confidence scale that the thinking and convinced braces include. The structure being defended is an ordinal one, and thus the braces can be moved as readers like. What matters are the relative thresholds: that thinking can involve a weaker degree of confidence than conviction, and both can involve a weaker degree of confidence than certainty.

The Lockean approach is elegant in its simplicity. However, the dominant view these days is that outright doxastic states cannot be reduced to confidence thresholds. The reason for this, as has frequently been pointed out, is that it's psychologically possible to be very confident that *p* even in *the absence of* a belief that *p*.[22] These lessons about the separability of belief and high confidence extend to thinking, conviction, and certainty.

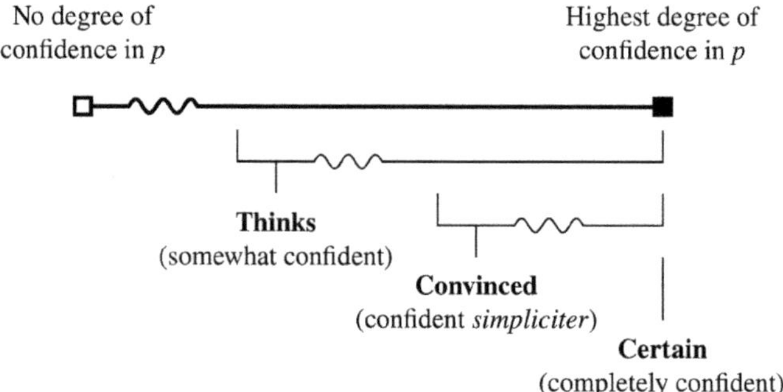

Figure 2 Lockean Threshold View.

[22] Williamson (2000:99), Clarke (2013:3–4), Buchak (2014:292), Ross and Schroeder (2014:286), Greco (2015), Staffel (2016), Friedman (2019), Weisberg (2020), Jackson (2020a,2020b), Bricker (2022), Clarke and Staffel (2023), Wedgwood (2023), Silva (2023a), and others defend the idea that high confidence shy of 1 can (and often *should*) come apart from belief in Lottery and many other cases of merely statistical evidence.

To see why many have regarded the separability of belief and high confidence as a datum to be accommodated, consider the following illustrative case:

> **Lottery**. Sam knows that the objective chances (L) *that his lottery ticket is a loser are 0.999*. Knowing these odds, his confidence that his ticket is a loser is high (but not maximal). But Sam also knows that there would be nothing abnormal should his ticket turn out to be a winner (Smith 2016) and that this could easily happen (Williamson 2000). In light of this, Sam is *not at all inclined to assert* that his ticket is a loser (not even to himself in his head), and Sam is *not at all inclined to act on* the claim that his ticket is a loser (e.g., by burning it or throwing it away), and Sam is *not at all inclined to treat that claim as a premise in deliberation* (at most he deliberates on the basis of the high probability of it being a loser). So there is, simply, no standard way in which Sam is inclined to treat L as true. So, *Sam does not believe L*. Nevertheless, when Sam learns that his ticket is a loser based on a news report, he is *utterly unsurprised*. And he is utterly unsurprised because *he was extremely confident that* that possible outcome – his having a losing ticket – would be the actual outcome.

Narratives such as this are intended to draw attention to a psychological possibility: high confidence states and belief states can come apart. Indeed, the case for separating belief and high confidence is provable, conditional on certain ways of characterizing both states. We'll discuss this further in Section 5.1.

Given that Lottery concerns the relation between *belief* and confidence levels, what relevance does this case have for theorizing about *thinking*, *conviction*, and *certainty*? Much. Recall that the judgement that Sam fails to believe that his ticket is a loser stems from the observation that Sam has no inclination to assert it, no inclination to act on it, and no inclination to use it in deliberation. But if Sam has no such inclinations, it's not only intuitive to think that Sam doesn't believe it, it's also intuitive to think that Sam doesn't think that it's true, is not convinced of it, and is not certain of it. We can add an argument to this intuition. For thinking, conviction, and certainty each entail belief (Section 7.2), and Sam's absent inclinations (dispositions) in Lottery preclude him from believing L on leading accounts of belief (Section 4.1). If right, then the absence of a belief in L entails the absence of these other outright doxastic states despite the presence of high confidence. If that's right, then the Lockean Threshold View should be rejected. Fortunately, T1–T8 are not without an explanation. A distinctively Kantian alternative awaits.

3 Degrees of Conviction and the Reduction of Outright States

The previous section examined the place of conviction *simpliciter* in relation to various outright doxastic states. But conviction also comes in degrees. This is something that seems to have been overlooked as a theoretically useful insight, for on the few occasions where epistemologists talk about 'degrees of conviction' they seem to use it synonymously with 'degree of belief', 'degree of confidence', or 'credences'.[23] This is a mistake. The concept of conviction is distinctive and holds the key to an alternative threshold view: a view of our outright attitudes characterized as threshold-exceeding states on an underlying scale that tracks **degrees of conviction** as opposed to **degrees of confidence**. The motivation for this is relatively straightforward: once we've seen that conviction comes in degrees, it's very hard to avoid the conclusion that being convinced *simpliciter* is just a matter of being convinced *to a sufficient degree*. Given what we learned in the previous section about how conviction *simpliciter* is logically related to thinking and certainty, a new threshold view presents itself.

3.1 Degrees of Conviction

Why think that there are degrees of conviction? Answer: our way of thinking and talking about conviction presupposes that there are degrees of conviction. We can easily make this point by considering cases. For context, assume that a trial is underway and you're a jury member assessing the evidence. In response to your growing body of evidence, you might well say any of the following in the course of the trial:

(14) ✓As the evidence increased, I became *increasingly convinced* that Morrison was guilty.

(14′) ✓*Je mehr sich die Hinweise häuften, desto mehr war ich (davon) überzeugt, dass Morrison schuldig ist.*

(15) ✓The more the evidence is overturned, the *less convinced* I become of Morrison's guilt.

(15′) ✓*Je mehr Hinweise widerlegt werden, desto weniger war ich von Morrisons Schuld überzeugt.*

(16) ✓I was *almost convinced* that Morrison was innocent, but then the cross-examination began.

(16′) ✓*Ich war fast (davon) überzeugt, dass Morrison unschuldig war, aber dann begann das Kreuzverhör.*

---

[23] For examples see White (2005:453–54), Beddor (2020:2), Holguín (2022:7), and Wedgwood (2023:ch.5).

(17) ✓I am (slightly) *less convinced* than I was that Morrison is guilty. However, *I remain convinced* that he's guilty.[24]

(17′) ✓*Ich bin [ein bisschen] weniger (davon) überzeugt, als ich es war, dass Morrison schuldig ist. Trotzdem bleibe ich (davon) überzeugt, dass er schuldig ist.*

(18) ✓I was convinced by the original evidence that Morrison committed the crime, but after his confession and the deep remorse he displayed while confessing, I became *completely (/totally/fully) convinced* that he committed the crime.

(18′) ✓*Ich war aufgrund der ursprünglichen Hinweise (davon) überzeugt, dass Morrison das Verbrechen begangen hat, aber nach seinem Geständnis und der tiefen Reue, die er während seines Geständnisses gezeigt hatte, war ich ganz [/total/vollkommen] (davon) überzeugt, dass er das Verbrechen begangen hat.*

The felicity of these statements tells us that 'convinced' is semantically gradable and connected to an underlying scale that tracks degrees of conviction.

Notice that (17) and (18) indicate that one can be convinced *simpliciter* and yet become more or less convinced, and also that one can be convinced *simpliciter* without being completely convinced. For a comparison consider 'wet': something can be wet *simpliciter* and become more or less wet. A shirt that has been splashed with a very large cup of water will be considered 'wet' by most ordinary standards. But if the shirt begins to dry it can become less wet without ceasing to be wet. Alternatively, if the shirt is splashed again with water it will become wetter, and if it's slowly submerged in water it will become even wetter. Whether a shirt has transitioned from being merely wet to being *completely* wet will depend on the contextually salient standard of precision.[25]

Notice also that the conviction scale has an uppermost point: being completely convinced. And this uppermost point is naturally identified with certainty. In evidence, consider separating them:

(19) #He's certain that she arrived, but he's not completely convinced that she arrived.

(19′) *#Er ist (sich) gewiss, dass sie angekommen ist, aber er ist nicht ganz (davon) überzeugt, dass sie angekommen ist.*

---

[24] Imagine you just had a significant piece of (apparent) evidence for Morrison's guilt overturned while the vast majority of evidence remained and continued to strongly support his guilt.

[25] See the end of Section 4.2 for more on standards of precision.

(20) #He's completely convinced that she arrived, but he's not certain that she arrived.

(20′) *#Er ist ganz (davon) überzeugt, dass sie angekommen ist, aber er ist (sich) nicht gewiss, dass sie angekommen ist.*

Once again, these sound awful.[26] And they sound awful, we think, because '*S* is certain that *p*' refers to the highest degree of conviction,[27] and vice versa.

Lastly, recall (16). Notice that the expression 'almost convinced' implies 'not convinced', just as 'almost dressed' implies 'not dressed' and 'almost wet' implies 'not wet'.[28] To say that one can be almost convinced despite failing to be convinced (*simpliciter*) is to say that one's degree of conviction can fail to be high enough to count as being convinced (*simpliciter*). A further observation about 'almost convinced' is that it implies 'at least somewhat convinced'. After all, if one were not at least somewhat convinced, one would be either: not at all convinced or close to it (=almost not at all convinced). And if one is either not at all convinced or close to it, one would not be almost convinced.[29] What would a situation look like where one is almost/somewhat convinced? Recall Diagnosis. There we observed a case where a doctor thinks that a patient has disease A because that is the most likely disease (52%) and also because it is the most typical disease for a patient to have in the given circumstances. We could easily imagine the same doctor saying: 'I'm at least somewhat convinced that the patient has disease A.'

At this point we are in a position to summarize the observations concerning natural language thresholds on the scale of conviction. They include:

- being completely convinced
- being sufficiently convinced to count as being convinced (*simpliciter*)
- being at least somewhat convinced
- being not at all convinced

All of these will become relevant in Section 3.2, and we'll say more about the nature of degrees of conviction in Sections 4 and 5.

---

[26] One native speaker suggested that 'gewiss' in (19′) can lend itself to an epistemic reading on which (19′) might be true. We intend the psychological reading.

[27] . . . relative to the contextually salient standard of precision. Again, see the end of Section 4.2 for more on this.

[28] For discussion see Rotstein and Winter (2004:265–67). Note that 'almost F' is not to be confused with 'could easily be F'. A very moist shirt can be almost wet even if one is in a desert and out of water, in which case it's false that the shirt could easily become wet.

[29] One can also test these implications with other non-complementary absolute gradable adjectives, for example, dressed/naked, wet/dry, hungry/satiated, sick/healthy. Tests should be sensitive to relevant degrees of precision. For other pairs, see Rotstein and Winter (2004:266), who also discuss 'almost' and 'slightly' modifiers with such adjectives. While 'somewhat' and 'slightly' are closely related modifiers, we have preferred 'somewhat' as it seems a little stronger and it provides very natural readings in the range of cases where we use it here and in Section 3.2. See also footnote 30.

3.2 The Kantian Threshold View

We can take each of the aforementioned regions on the degree of conviction scale and connect them to the outright doxastic states discussed in Section 2.2, as indicated in Figure 3.

Section 3.1 provided semantic motivations for identifying certainty with being completely convinced, that is, the state picked out by the endpoint on the conviction scale. Similar semantic motivations are available for identifying conviction – that is, the state of being convinced – with having a sufficiently high degree of conviction. After all, it makes no sense to think of oneself or others as being convinced that *p*, while not being convinced that *p* to a sufficiently high degree. Moreover, since one can be convinced without being certain (Section 2.2), the degree of conviction required for being convinced must be a degree that falls short of complete conviction.

Where does thinking lie on this scale? Well, we saw that one can think that *p* without being convinced that *p* (Section 2.2). So if thinking has a place on the conviction scale, its lower boundary must be below the lower boundary required for being convinced. Further semantic considerations suggest that thinking's lower-boundary lies with *being at least somewhat convinced*. In favour of this, consider the questionable felicity of the following conjunctions:

(21) #She thinks that *p*, but she is not even somewhat convinced that *p*.
(21′) *#Sie denkt, dass p, aber sie ist nicht einmal ansatzweise (davon) überzeugt, dass p.*

(22) #She's somewhat convinced that *p*, but she doesn't think that *p*.
(22′) *#Sie ist einigermaßen (davon) überzeugt, dass p, aber sie denkt nicht, dass p.*

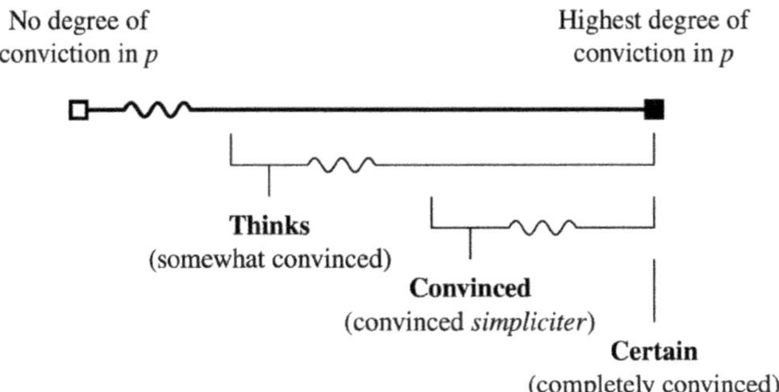

Figure 3 Kantian Threshold View.

Try and imagine yourself saying such things. For example: 'I think she's on her way, but I'm not even somewhat convinced that she's on her way', or 'I'm somewhat convinced that she's on her way, but I don't think she's on her way'. These sound bizarre. And we cannot easily interpret such statements just in terms of sentence meaning.

The neg-raising behaviour of 'thinks' (Section 2.2) may provide additional evidence for connecting thinking and being at least somewhat convinced, for the expression 'at least somewhat convinced' seems to neg-raise. For example, uses of 'he is not even somewhat convinced that she's home' tends to suggest that 'he is somewhat convinced that she's not home'. Altogether, we have non-trivial evidence for the following explanation of these facts:

> **T=SC** Necessarily, *S* thinks that *p* iff *S* is at least somewhat convinced that *p*. *Notwendigerweise gilt, S denkt, dass p, genau dann, wenn S wenigstens einigermaßen (davon) überzeugt ist, dass p.*[30]

Figure 3, in addition to encoding T=SC, also represents the idea that thinking's lower boundary should not be too close to the zero-degree endpoint. But remember that the absolute placement of these thresholds is irrelevant to our purposes. They can be moved. What does matter is their relative location: thinking can involve a *lower* degree of conviction than being convinced, and both can involve a *lower* degree of conviction than certainty.

[30] Some may want to bring thinking's lower boundary down closer to the zero-degree endpoint. For motivation see Holguín (2022). The identification of thinking with being at least somewhat convinced might be consistent with this to some extent. But there is a limit, for when *F* (*simpliciter*) is a strong threshold property (a property that marks a threshold far from the zero-degree endpoint – for example, 'tall', 'heavy', 'dangerous', and 'rough' – 'somewhat *F*' implies a degree of the underlying property tracked by the relevant scale that *gets acceptably close to F* (*simpliciter*) and thus opens up a notable gap between being somewhat *F* and regions closer to the zero-degree point – for example, 'short', 'light', 'almost safe', 'almost smooth'. This seems to hold for many relative and partial absolute gradable adjectives. For example, a single-storey building, even though it has some degree of height, does not count as being 'somewhat tall' when the relevant comparison class is skyscrapers. After all, this kind of building will be classified as 'short', and 'short' and 'somewhat tall' seem mutually exclusive (when the reference class is held fixed). Similarly, a soccer league's games might involve such a small degree of danger of physical harm that we count it as 'almost safe'. We would not ordinarily go on to classify those same games as being *somewhat dangerous* just because they have a non-zero associated degree of danger (while holding the relevant degree of precision associated with the scale fixed). So 'almost safe' and 'somewhat dangerous' *seem* mutually exclusive, and a ready explanation is that when *F* (*simpliciter*) picks out a strong threshold property, 'somewhat *F*' implies a degree of the underlying property that gets acceptably close to *F* (*simpliciter*) and therefore requires a notable gap between it and the zero-degree endpoint. So take the following attractive ideas: (i) it's natural to associate thinking with being at least somewhat convinced, (ii) 'convinced' is strong, and (iii) 'at least somewhat *F*' when '*F*' is strong opens up a gap in relation to the lower end of the scale. These jointly suggest that the zero-degree endpoint on the conviction scale and thinking's lower boundary cannot be too close together. This is represented in Figure 3. But again, there is room to debate how wide the gap should be and whether it should remain at least proportionally fixed across contexts and relative to different degrees of precision.

Notice how the scalar structure in Figure 3 helps model the facts of Section 2.2:

T1 It is possible that *S* thinks that *p*, but *S* is not certain that *p*.
In the model, every point within the thinking region that is shy of the endpoint is a point that represents thinking without certainty.

T2 Necessarily, if *S* is certain that *p*, then *S* thinks that *p*.
In the model, to be at the certainty endpoint just is to be at one point within the thinking region.

T3 Necessarily, if *S* is convinced that *p*, then *S* thinks that *p*.
In the model, every point in the conviction region is a point within the thinking region.

T4 Necessarily, if *S* is certain that *p*, then *S* is convinced that *p*.
In the model, the certainty endpoint is always within the conviction region.

T6 It is possible that *S* thinks that *p*, but *S* is not convinced that *p*.
In the model, there are points within the thinking region that are not within the conviction region.

T8 It is possible that *S* is convinced that *p*, but *S* is not certain that *p*.
In the model, there are points within the conviction region that fall short of the certainty endpoint.

This is all very tidy. And just as with the Lockean Threshold View, the Kantian Threshold View provides an equally tidy explanation of T5 (=thinking is normatively weaker than conviction) and T7 (=conviction and certainty are not as normatively weak as thinking). We need only avail ourselves of the epistemological principle that we are required to proportion our degree of conviction to the strength of our evidence.[31]

4 The Metaphysics of Belief and Degrees of Conviction

The previous section provided reasons for thinking that there exist degrees of conviction and that we can reduce thinking, conviction, and certainty to degrees of conviction that exceed certain thresholds. The central project of this section is to develop a metaphysical account of degrees of conviction.

[31] See Silva (2023b:ch.7) for defence of evidentialism in the face of the common externalist challenge from basic/animal knowledge. We are aware that epistemological matters become more complicated once we've identified two kinds of degreed doxastic states: degrees of conviction and degrees of confidence (Section 5.1). Since our aim in this volume is to better understand the metaphysics of the mind we set these epistemological issues aside. For relevant discussions of different kinds of evidential support that could be segued into a discussion of what evidence impacts these different states, see Jackson (2020a) and Smith (2016).

The account of degrees of conviction to follow stems from the connection between conviction, belief, and a prominent body of research that takes belief to be, at least partially, a dispositional state. We'll explore a well-motivated framework in which one's degree of conviction just is, roughly, the degree to which one is disposed to rely on *p*.

4.1 What Is Belief?

Recent analytic philosophy has had a lot to say about the nature of belief. While there is a good bit of controversy here, there is a widely shared idea that believing that *p* is at least partially connected to *reliance-dispositions*: dispositions to rely on *p* in certain ways when it comes to situations in which one takes *p* to be relevant.

In evidence, consider the widely endorsed representationalist–functionalist model of belief in the philosophy of mind. As Lyons (2009:71) describes this view: believing that *p* is 'a matter of standing in a certain functional relation to a representation, *R*, which has the content that *p*,' where the relevant functional relation involving the representation *R* is such that '*R* is *poised* to have [=disposed to have] the causal role definitive of belief: *R* is used as a premise for inference, for practical syllogisms, and the like (Field 1978; Fodor 1990)' (emphasis added). Further connecting belief to reliance-dispositions, Stalnaker (1984:15) says that 'to believe [*p*] is to be *disposed to* act in ways that would tend to satisfy one's desires, whatever they are, in a world in which *p* (together with one's other beliefs) were true' (emphasis added). Zimmerman (2018:1) writes: 'To believe something at a given time is to be so *disposed* that you would use that information to guide those relatively attentive and self-controlled activities you might engage in at that time, whether these activities involve bodily movement or not' (emphasis added). Ross and Schroeder (2014:267–8) argue that 'at least part of the functional role of belief is that believing that *p* defeasibly *disposes* the believer to treat *p* as true in her [practical and theoretical] reasoning' (emphasis added; cf. Frankish 2009; Wedgwood 2023). Also emphasizing the dispositional character of belief, Weisberg (2020:4) writes of two principal characteristics of belief: 'First, [in believing *p*] we become *disposed* to rely on *p* – to use it as a premise in future reasoning, to assume it in decision-making, and to assert it. . . . Second, we become resistant to [=*disposed* to resist] reopening deliberation – we treat the question whether *p* as settled' (emphasis added). Schwitzgebel (2002) characterizes belief as a dispositional state involving certain behavioural dispositions (dispositions to act and assert), certain cognitive dispositions (dispositions to infer), and certain affective dispositions (the disposition to feel surprise should one's belief turn out false). There are also knowledge-first characterizations of the dispositional nature of belief: Hyman (2017:284) writes that 'we can define the belief that *p* . . . as the *disposition* to act (think, feel) as one would if one knew that *p*' (emphasis added; cf. Williamson 2000; McGrath 2021b:175). Leitgeb (2017:70–2) points out that this broadly dispositional vision of belief is not only a credible commitment of contemporary epistemology and philosophy of mind, but it's also attested to in the history of philosophy, especially in Hume. Section 7 provides evidence that Kant too would have been amenable to a broadly dispositional theory of belief.

We'll capture the idea that *some* set of reliance-dispositions are, at least partially, constitutive of belief as follows:

> **Minimal Nature**. At least part of what it is to believe that *p* is to have a disposition to rely on *p* in the ways required for belief when *p* is taken to be relevant.[32]

A few points of clarification. First, the intended idea of *relying on p* is not simply the idea of *using* the proposition *p*. One can use the proposition *p* in suppositional reasoning even while rejecting *p*. One can also use the proposition *p* in at least a derivative sense when one uses the proposition *that p is very probable* in one's reasoning. But when one relies on *p* by, for example, asserting *that p*, acting *on p*, and treating *p* as a premise when aiming to form beliefs about what one ought to do and think, one is relying on *p as though it were true*. It is unsurprising, then, that we find many characterizing believing that *p* as: treating /holding /taking /regarding *p* as true.[33]

Second, the idea of 'taking *p* to be relevant' is what we think the relevant *stimulus condition* is for triggering a belief's constitutive dispositions. For an analogy take fragility: the disposition to break *when struck*. Not every fragile glass breaks. It's the striking that triggers its disposition to break. In what follows, 'taking *p* to be relevant' is the stimulus condition for belief and it will be left unanalysed. For however it is analysed, it's very clear that we do take some propositions, and not others, to be relevant when it comes to what to do and to think on particular occasions.[34]

Lastly, the expression 'the ways required for belief' is to be filled in with the sorts of ways talked about here in regard to assertion, action, or

[32] Even in an interpretivist view of belief, one would not likely interpret an individual as having a belief unless one were willing to interpret the individual as having some set of dispositions that could be interpreted as reliance-dispositions. See Schwitzgebel (2023) for interpretivist references.

[33] See Crane (2013), Clarke and Staffel (2023), and Schwitzgebel (2023).

[34] For example, while we believe that the moon is not made of cheese, this did not figure in our deliberations, assertions, and actions in the last few days. Why? Because it was not a proposition we took to be relevant in the last few days.

deliberation. Since different theorists may have different preferences here, we've elected to use the neutral 'ways required for belief' that you may fill in as you like. But to give us something concrete to work with we will sometimes make reference to the following instance of Minimal Nature:

> **Minimal Nature + Assertion + Action + Deliberation (MAD)**: At least part of what it is for an agent *S* to believe that *p* is for *S* to have a disposition to assert that *p*, or to act on *p*, or to treat *p* as a premise in deliberation when *S* takes the proposition *p* to be relevant.

MAD is a sane characterization of belief. As noted above, the reliance-dispositions connected to belief are often thought to involve action, assertion, and deliberation. After all, it would be entirely natural to characterize someone as believing that the train station is nearby, if, when taking that claim to be relevant, one had a disposition to assert that claim, to act on it, and to rely on it in deliberation. Furthermore, if someone lacked all three of those dispositions, it would be entirely odd to claim that they believe that the train station is nearby. Many of those cited earlier in this section would agree. But there are subtleties here. For example, clearly one might have a stronger disposition to assert *p* than to act on *p*. One might also have a disposition to assert that *p* while lacking a disposition to deliberate with *p*. Such dispositional misalignments are probably not uncommon. So we could get more fine-grained than MAD. But MAD is nice to work with. It lets us count someone as a believer just so long as they are disposed to have *at least one* of the noted responses when taking *p* to be relevant. Perhaps that's too low a bar for belief. So bear in mind that MAD is being put forward only as a toy instance of Minimal Nature. Readers unsympathetic to MAD are welcome to substitute their own instance of Minimal Nature in what follows.

4.2 From Belief's Dispositions to Degrees of Conviction

What is belief's relation to assent, thinking, conviction, and certainty? Here are four ways of connecting belief to these states:

> **B=C$_{\mathbf{ert}}$** Belief just is certainty.
> **B=C** Belief just is conviction.
> **B=T** Belief just is thinking.
> **B=A** Belief just is assent (*Fürwahrhalten*, i.e., holding for true).

B=C$_{ert}$ is manifestly implausible. We know none who defend it. Some have explicitly argued for B=T.[35] In his work on Kant's epistemology, Chignell (2007a, 2007b) has argued that contemporary uses of 'belief' shouldn't be taken

[35] Hawthorne et al. (2016), Dorst (2019), Rothschild (2020), and Holguín (2022).

to refer to assent or opinion, and he comes close to explicitly endorsing B=C.[36] Crane (2013:164) has advocated B=A and Schwitzgebel (2023) suggests that this is the dominant position among contemporary philosophers of mind.[37] We'll provide arguments that favour B=A in Section 7.2. But so long as at least one of these views is true and the Kantian Threshold View is correct, we can leverage insights about the dispositional nature of belief to provide us with insights about degrees of conviction.

Here's the logic of this move. The Kantian Threshold View tells us that thinking, conviction, and certainty are just sufficiently strong degrees of conviction. So any deep metaphysical connection between belief and these threshold states will license some inferences about the nature of degrees of conviction from information we have about the dispositional nature of belief. B=C_{ert}, B=C, and B=T identify belief with some degree of conviction threshold, and thus provide a strong metaphysical basis for theorizing about degrees of conviction in terms of belief's dispositions. Leveraging B=A requires collateral premises because the Kantian Threshold View says nothing about assent. Recall 'assenting to *p*' expresses the concept of *taking p to be the case/holding p as true*. Next, notice that thinking, being convinced, and being certain that *p* seem to *constitutively* involve the idea of taking it to be the case that *p*; that is, at least part of what it is to think, be convinced, or be certain that *p* is to take it to be the case that *p*. So if both B=A and this partial constitutive claim are true (Section 7.2), then there are metaphysical reasons to move from facts about the dispositional nature of belief/assent to facts about degrees of conviction.

As we aim to unpack degrees of conviction in terms of degreed facts about belief's dispositions, we need to say something about the structure of dispositions in general. Part of what is involved in having a disposition is for one to respond in a certain way across a given set of possibilities. This is true whether or not one prefers a counterfactual account of dispositions or a version of the modal-proportional approach. The latter approach has become an increasingly prominent approach to the modal structure of dispositions and can be presented thus:

> **Dispositional Proportionality Principle**: Necessarily, *x* has a disposition to φ when stimulus condition *c* obtains if and only if *x* φs in a sufficiently high proportion of *the relevant* worlds where *c* obtains.[38]

---

[36] Chignell has expressed a tentative preference for B=C in personal conversation. Smithies (2023) comes close to this too, though he connects belief to *phenomenal conviction*. See Section 5.2.

[37] Schwitzgebel (2023) remarks that 'Anglophone philosophers of mind generally use the term "belief" to refer to the attitude we have, roughly, whenever we take something to be the case or regard it as true.' See also Staffel's remarks in Clarke and Staffel (2023:§2).

[38] Advocates of modal-proportional approaches fine-tune their preferred version of this principle. So this principle is offered as a modest idealization of an in-house debate among these disposition theorists. See Manley and Wasserman (2007:72; 2008:76; 2011), Vetter (2015:ch.3–5),

As has been pointed out by advocates of such accounts, the right-hand side of this principle needn't be understood as providing a reductive analysis of dispositions nor as providing grounding conditions that partially explain why an object has a given disposition. It is perfectly fine, and surely more intuitive, to treat the left-hand side as more fundamental. What is important for our purposes is that having a disposition tells us something about the structure of modal space.

Notice that when it comes to assessing whether x has a disposition to φ, the Dispositional Proportionality Principle has us focus on the *relevant* worlds where x exists and its stimulus condition c obtains. So which worlds are relevant? Manley and Wasserman (2008) and other disposition theorists suggest that the relevant worlds should be restricted to worlds where the laws of nature remain the same. They also argue that the relevant worlds should be restricted to worlds where *all* the intrinsic properties of x remain the same. For example, they write that when it comes to determining an object's dispositions, 'we consider what objects would do under various extrinsic conditions in which they are (at the outset) as they actually are intrinsically' (76). This particular restriction generates a potential disconnect between how at least some advocates of versions of the Dispositional Proportionality Principle would have us understand dispositions and how moral philosophers and epistemologists have thought about the dispositions associated with prominent moral and epistemic virtues (generosity, love, reliability, and so forth). The problem is superficial, but requires attention. We'll come back to this later in this section.

Let's first look at the mechanics of the Dispositional Proportionality Principle. Take fragility. A fragile glass is a glass that is disposed to break when struck. What does that involve? According to this principle, it involves the glass breaking in a *sufficiently high proportion* of worlds where: (i) it is struck, (ii) the laws of nature remain the same, and (iii) all of the glass's intrinsic properties remain the same. The 'sufficiently' qualification is important because breaking in *some very small proportion of worlds* is not enough to be fragile. The proportion has to be sufficiently high, where 'sufficiently high' is determined by the kind of object in question, the kind of disposition in question, and contextually salient standards that can shift the sufficiency threshold.[39]

Aimar (2019). See also Friend and Kimpton-Nye (2023:28–33). For others who work with a streamlined principle like this see Beddor and Pavese (2020:66–67).

[39] For example, compare a fragile wine glass with a concrete block that is declared fragile due to poor mixing when in its liquid form. The fragile concrete block will break in a much smaller proportion of worlds when struck than the fragile wine glass. But even so, the concrete block counts as fragile because the contextually relevant standard of fragility is set by well-made concrete blocks, which will break in a much smaller proportion of cases than properly produced concrete blocks.

Among the advantages of modal views of dispositions is that they can be easily leveraged to explain *the fact that dispositions come in degrees*. As Manley and Wasserman (2007) point out: it is clearly possible for there to be two fragile glasses, g_1 and g_2, such that g_1 is more fragile than g_2. That is, g_1 has *a stronger disposition to break when struck* than g_2. On modal views, this amounts to saying that *the proportion* of relevant worlds where g_1 is struck and breaks is *larger than the proportion* of such worlds where g_2 is struck and breaks.[40]

Back to belief. Take a normal, mature, human thinker, Sam, in the following possible situation:

PS: At time *t*, Sam looks into his wallet and sees only ten euros in it.

Does Sam believe the proposition (M) *that he has only ten euros in his wallet*? To answer this, let us consider situations that seem relevant for whether or not we ascribe to Sam a belief in M:

PS1: Shortly after *t*, *Sam runs into his mother who asks to borrow five euros* and Sam thereby comes to take M to be relevant. To what extent does Sam rely on M (e.g., in terms of assertion, action, and deliberation) across (relevant) possible worlds where this situation occurs? For example, does he rely on M across a large, or medium, or small, or very small proportion of these possible situations?

PS2: Shortly after *t*, *Sam goes shopping and is asked to pay for an item costing nine euros* and thereby comes to take M to be relevant. To what extent does Sam rely on M across (relevant) possible worlds where this situation occurs?

PS3: Shortly after *t*, *Sam starts thinking about unrelated issues and randomly considers the question whether M is true* and thereby comes to take M to be relevant. To what extent does Sam rely on M across (relevant) possible worlds where this situation occurs?

PS4: Shortly after *t*, *someone juggling and wearing a bear costume asks Sam if he has any money* and he thereby comes to take M to be relevant. To what extent does Sam rely on M across (relevant) possible worlds where this situation occurs?

PSn: . . . and so on . . .

The set of possible situations is vast and involves situations stranger than PS4. But, provided Sam's apparent evidence for M does not change across

[40] See Manley and Wasserman (2007) and Vetter (2015:ch.3).

PS1–PSn we have the clear sense that if Sam is a typical human with only typical levels of irrationality, he will rely on M in assertion, action, and deliberation across a reasonably large proportion of those possible situations, including PS1–PS4. *And if we were convinced otherwise, we would tend to reject the idea that Sam believes M.* In this way, believing *p* is like loving your spouse. Loving your spouse is partially a matter of being disposed to act on behalf of your spouse. But we would never say that you love your spouse if you act on their behalf *only when* in a very narrow range of circumstances, for example, only when you've had two cocktails, and you're in a good mood, and you're well rested, and you have absolutely nothing pressing on you mind, and you believe it's a leap year. The disposition to act on behalf of your spouse that we intuitively associate with loving them involves acting on their behalf across a much broader range of possible circumstances. So too with our ordinary concept of belief.

This point about the range of circumstances associated with belief's dispositions requires that when it comes to assessing whether an agent believes *p* at *t* we do not look only at how they behave in cases where their intrinsic states – for example, their mental states – are exactly as they are at *t*. For example, in each of PS1–PS4 there are all kinds of mental states of Sam's *that change* as he becomes perceptually aware of the many changes in his immediate environment. What this demands is a more inclusive account of *the relevant worlds* than we find in Manley and Wasserman (2007,2008), whose view involves holding *all* of an individual's intrinsic features fixed. That the relevant worlds for many agential dispositions should be more inclusive by allowing for some changes to an agent's intrinsic features is an entrenched presupposition when thinking about the dispositions associated with our knowledge-producing capacities.[41]

What, then, might the relevant worlds be when it comes to assessing whether someone holds a belief? There is room to disagree over optimal answers to this question. But to get the conversation going let's note a heuristic for answering this question. First, consider paradigmatic cases where we would ascribe a belief to an agent at a time *t*. Next, look at the sorts of possible changes to

[41] For example, Crane (2013:164–6) writes that 'it is essential to beliefs that they persist through changes in current consciousness' and therefore persist through changes in an individual's intrinsic states. Leitgeb (2017:72–3) expands on the same point. Sosa (2015:95–8) argues that knowledge-yielding competences are dispositions to succeed in forming true beliefs across a sufficient proportion of relevant worlds, where the relevant worlds involve restrictions to a 'seat', a 'shape', and a space of 'situations'. Notably, he does *not* restrict the worlds relevant for assessing whether one has a disposition to form a true belief at *t* to a set of worlds where *all* of an agent's intrinsic features remain *exactly* as they are at *t*. See also Greco (2010), and Beddor and Pavese (2020). For discussions in moral psychology that treat the dispositions constitutive of our character traits (e.g., shyness, generosity, humility, and so on) in ways that do not appear to require that all intrinsic states be held fixed, see Miller (2014) and references therein.

an agent's intrinsic properties that would or would not make a difference to whether or not we would continue to ascribe the belief to the agent *at t*. With that as a guiding idea, here is an answer that attracts us:

> **Belief's Modal Base of Worlds (BMW).** The relevant worlds for assessing whether or not *S* believes that *p* (/has a disposition to rely on *p* in the ways constitutive of belief) at time *t* in a world *w*, are the worlds where:
>
> (i) *S* takes *p* to be relevant, and
> (ii) the laws of nature remain as they are at *t* in *w*, and
> (iii) *S*'s internal cognitive processes are as they are at *t* in *w*, and
> (iv) *S*'s apparent evidence for *p* includes the apparent evidence *S* has for *p* at *t* in *w*, and
> (v) *S*'s apparent evidence for *p* appears to support *p* at least as much as it does at *t* in *w*.[42]

The need for conditions (i) and (ii) have been noted. Condition (iii) has us exclude worlds where *S* processes incoming information very differently than she does in *w* at *t*. For example, it has us exclude cases where *S* in *w* at *t* processes information like we do, but then later endures psychological conditioning or manipulation that causes her, say, to treat occurrent smells as evidence of facts about ancient history or to treat tautologies as conclusive evidence for arbitrary contingent claims. Intuitively, worlds where one processes information very differently from how one actually does in *w* at *t* seem irrelevant to whether or not one believes *p* in *w* at *t*. Perhaps some small differences in one's cognitive processes should be allowed here. If so, this will be one dimension along which borderline cases can be developed. But borderline cases are inevitable.

Condition (iv) has us hold fixed, for example, an agent's *apparent* memories in so far as they seem to have an evidential bearing on whether *p*. But this condition allows the agent to undergo new experiences and acquire new apparent memories. The motivation for this condition is the obvious fact that a loss of apparent evidence for *p* can change whether we believe *p*. So we want to hold one's apparent evidence fixed when looking at the worlds relevant for assessing whether or not one believes that *p* at *t*.

Condition (v) screens off worlds where newly acquired apparent evidence appears to undermine *p*. For example, suppose at *t* Sam sees that he's in a room and comes to believe (R) *that he's in a room*. But just after that, at *t+*, Sam walks

---

[42] We take one's apparent evidence to be evidence 'from one's point of view'. What is that? One could take a view like Schroeder's (2015) on which one's apparent evidence (subjective reasons) are the contents of one's representational states. For alternative characterizations of apparent evidence see Sylvan (2015) and references therein.

out of the room into broad daylight. After walking out of the room he will have no disposition to act, assert, or deliberate on R. But his newly acquired apparent evidence has also shifted as he's now having a normal perceptual experience of being outside in the sun. Sam now has a very different body of evidence bearing on R: a body of apparent evidence that no longer seems to him to support R. But we would not count Sam's failure to rely on R *upon walking outside* against the idea that Sam believed R *before* walking outside when his apparent evidence continued to appear to support R.

All together, conditions (i)–(v) only ask us to hold fixed a proper subset of an agent's intrinsic properties across worlds where they exist. We want to emphasize that what follows depends on Minimal Nature (and not MAD) and a version of the Dispositional Proportionality Principle (and not the particular way of identifying the relevant worlds found in BMW). We offer MAD and BMW because they seem reasonably close to correct. Unsympathetic readers are free to refine both MAD and BMW as they see fit.

Now we are in a position to provide an account of degrees of reliance:

> **Degrees of Reliance**. An agent's degree of reliance on *p* is determined by the proportion of relevant worlds (e.g., as specified in BMW) in which the agent relies on *p* in whatever ways are required for belief (e.g., as specified in MAD). The stronger the proportion of relevant worlds in which the agent relies on *p*, the stronger the degree of reliance.

One advantage of this proposal is that one's degree of reliance can be represented as a rational number expressed as a fraction *n/m*, where *n* is the set of relevant worlds where one relies on *p* when one takes the proposition *p* to be relevant, and where *m* is the total set of relevant worlds where one takes the proposition *p* to be relevant.[43] We will not get into the business of assigning numerical values, or measures over infinite sets of relevant worlds. We are here piggybacking off the yeoman work of modal theorists of dispositions who have explicitly analysed dispositions and their degrees in terms of proportionality over infinite sets of worlds. Further, the challenges of fixing numerical values here are no more daunting or more demanding than they are in familiar Bayesian frameworks.

The Kantian Threshold View sketched in Section 3 reduces the outright doxastic states of thinking, conviction, and certainty to degrees of conviction. But that does not itself tell us what degrees of conviction are. So what are degrees of conviction? Provided that 'belief' as used in contemporary

[43] Bayesians should not be too quickly overjoyed by this for reasons noted in Section 5.1.

philosophy of mind and epistemology refers to either assent, or conviction, or thinking, we suggest the following:

> **Degrees of Conviction (DoC)**: *S*'s degree of conviction in *p* just is the proportion of relevant worlds in which *S* relies on *p* in whatever ways are required for belief when *S* takes the proposition *p* to be relevant.[44]

That is, degrees of conviction are just degrees of reliance. It is difficult to find reason to reject this without either rejecting (i) the idea that 'belief' (as standardly used) refers either to assent, or to thinking, or to conviction, or else rejecting (ii) Minimal Nature, that is, that belief constitutively involves reliance-dispositions.[45]

One thing to bear in mind is that this account of degrees of conviction papers over the psychological complexity noted at the end of Section 4.1. For if belief is associated with multiple ways of relying on *p*, then we can contrast the proportion of worlds in which one relies on *p* in one way, w_1, with the proportion of worlds in which one relies on *p* in other ways, w_2 or w_3. So if belief involves a disposition to rely on *p* in multiple ways, then there can be a further measurable qualitative difference between agents who, according to DoC, are both convinced of *p* to *the same degree*. This point merits exploration that we cannot provide here.

There are further types of degreed doxastic states that we need to discuss to help us see the distinctiveness of DoC. This is the topic of Section 5. Before turning to that there are some final matters to discuss concerning the regions near the extreme ends of the degree of conviction scale. First, recall Figure 3 from Section 3.2. You'll notice a gap between thinking's lower boundary and the zero-degree endpoint. You may begin to wonder whether there's anything worth calling a 'degree of conviction' in that gap, especially as one gets close to the zero point. We think so. Again, following Manley and Wasserman (2007:73), let fragility be our model. Consider two non-fragile concrete blocks, that is, both blocks *lack* a disposition to break when struck. Even though both blocks lack

---

44 It is noteworthy that Schulz (2021a,2021b) has developed a very similar account of degrees of 'outright belief' stemming from cases inspired by remarks of Williamson (2000:99). If one were to identify Schulz's use of the term 'outright belief' with conviction, then we would have defended very similar conclusions. As we see it, our projects principally differ in the *kind* of argument being provided for these similar conclusions. Ours proceeds from attention to the use of graded and ungraded doxastic terms in natural languages as well as the literature on belief's dispositions. Schulz's arguments stem principally from an attempt to leverage a semi-technical notion of 'outright belief'. See footnote 10.

45 Some have opposed the use of dispositions to account for degrees of confidence (credences), for example, Eriksson and Hájek (2007). However, credences are not degrees of conviction (Section 5.1). Further, it's unclear to what extent their opposition to dispositional accounts of credences survive subsequent work on the nature of dispositions, how to account for masks, mimics, finks, and reverse-finks of dispositions (see references to recent work supporting the Dispositional Proportionality Principle), and recent work on the context sensitivity of gradable ascriptions (see the comments on the Lewis–Unger debate in this section).

fragility *simpliciter*, one may yet be 'more fragile' than the other in the sense that one breaks in *more* striking cases than the other. So while we should not think that in that gap in Figure 3 there is a disposition to rely on *p simpliciter*, there are in that gap degrees of that which makes (or at least marks) such a disposition: possible cases where one takes *p* to be relevant and then relies on *p*. The more such cases, the stronger the degree of reliance/conviction. It is only when the proportion is large enough that one will count as having a disposition *simpliciter* to rely on *p* when *p* is taken to be relevant (cf. Vetter 2015:ch.3).

Second, when it comes to degrees of conviction, how large a proportion of worlds is needed to reach a degree of conviction sufficient for being certain (=completely convinced)? It's a good question, and a hard one. Certainty is, as Unger (1975:ch.2) argued, an *absolute term*. You are certain, said Unger, just in case you are 'not at all in doubt', or as we've been putting it 'completely convinced'. Does that mean that psychological certainty requires that there exist no relevant worlds where you fail to rely on *p*? Unger would have said 'Yes'. But Lewis (1979:353–4) argued that we should not expect a *fixed* upper bound with many absolute terms; rather, we should expect a *flexible* upper bound. To see the motivation for a flexible Lewisian account consider the absolute term 'flat'. To call something 'flat' is to say, roughly, that it's not at all bumpy, bent, or crooked. What do we regard as standard cases of 'flat' objects? The desks that populate our libraries and offices, the screens of our computers, and many other ordinary objects. But zoom in close enough to any of these and you'll find some bumps, bends, and crookedness. So these are not flat objects? 'No!' says Lewis. They are flat ... according to a somewhat undemanding, contextually salient standard of precision. Many linguists agree with Lewis.[46] Arguably, then, certainty doesn't require one to rely on *p* in *every* relevant world where they take *p* to be relevant. One need only do so in *enough* relevant worlds, where the proportion of worlds required to be 'enough' can expand or shrink depending on the contextually salient standard of precision.

Third, the previous point about degrees of precision concerned the upper end of the conviction scale. But what about degrees of precision and the bottom end? Again, we should allow for some flexibility there too as the contextually salient standard of precision might allow one to count as being not at all convinced that *p* while still relying on *p* in a sufficiently small proportion of worlds.

Lastly, it should be noted that *lacking* a disposition to rely on *p* need have no impact on whether one *has* a disposition to rely on $\neg p$. One can lack both

[46] For more on imprecision generally, see Lakoff (1973), Sadock (1977), Krifka (2002,2007), and Sauerland and Stateva (2007). For imprecision as it relates to absolute gradable adjectives, see Pinkal (1995) and Kennedy (2007). Thanks to Wes Siscoe for pointing this out.

dispositions. So being not at all convinced that *p* does not entail thinking/being at least somewhat convinced that $\neg p$.

5 The *Sui Generity* of Degrees of Conviction

Sections 2 and 3 argued that thinking (opinion), conviction, and certainty should be understood in terms of thresholds on a scale that tracks degrees of conviction. Section 4 provided a metaphysical theory of degrees of conviction in terms of degrees of reliance. But how do degrees of conviction relate to other degreed states such as degrees of confidence (credences), degrees of felt conviction, degrees of revisability, and usual characterizations of degrees of belief? This section explains the distinctiveness of degrees of conviction in relation to each of these other states.

5.1 Degrees of Conviction Are Not Degrees of Confidence (Credences)

Degrees of confidence are among our doxastic states. Sometimes we refer to these with the term 'credences', though at other times the term 'credences' is used to refer to *representations of* an agent's mental states in a formal model, for example, in a Bayesian model.[47] We are not here concerned with formal representations of our mental states, but relations among the states themselves. Additionally, 'degrees of confidence' will always refer to *non-phenomenal* degrees of confidence. That is, we are not concerned with the experience of feeling confident, but with confidence states that are connected to behaviour.

To get a sense of behavioural ways of understanding confidence, consider Greco's (2015) distinction between asserting that *p* and *hedged assertions* of *p*:

> We can distinguish outright, unqualified assertions from assertions that are 'hedged' in various ways. Consider the following schematic examples:
>
> 1. More likely than not, *p*
> 2. Very probably, *p*
> 3. With at least 99% probability, *p*
> 4. *p*
>
> Whatever sentence we plug in for *p*, 1–4 will [when asserted] naturally be heard as expressing increasing levels of confidence. (Greco 2015:182)

Assertions of 1–3 are speech acts that put forward $\neg p$ as a possibility at the same time as they put forward *p* as the dominant possibility. In addition to hedged assertion we have *hedged deliberation*, that is, deliberation that treats only qualified claims like 1–3 as premises in deciding what to do or to think.

[47] See Staffel's contribution in Clark and Staffel (2023).

Further, we have *hedged actions*. For example, suppose one's sole desire is to make as much money as possible by risking up to 100 euros on whether outcome *o* obtains. Then, bets short of 100 euros (but greater than zero euros) on *o* may be thought of as ways of performing a *hedged action*, where the more one will bet on *o* the more confident one is in *o*.

These characterizations of hedged activities help us understand the functional role of (non-maximal) confidence. *But note: it's not yet a full theory, much less an analysis, of what degrees of confidence are*. We will not provide such a theory in what follows. Rather, we will rely on facts that confidence theorists have widely taken to be obvious about degrees of confidence and then use those facts to distinguish degrees of confidence from degrees of conviction.[48]

Could degrees of conviction be the very same thing as degrees of confidence (credences)? This question brings us back to the following idea:

> **Conviction–Confidence Identity**. Degrees of conviction just are degrees of confidence.

The first problem with this stems from the Lottery case of Section 2.3. There we highlighted how many maintain that there are possible cases in which the following two conditions hold:

> **High**. *S* has a high, but non-maximal, confidence that *p* at *t*.
> **No**. *S* does not believe that *p* at *t*.

Now, if *S* fails to believe that *p*, then *S* must have a *low* degree of conviction. This follows from the idea that belief is to be identified with either thinking, or conviction, or assent (Section 4.2), and that these states are just a matter of having a sufficiently high degree of conviction (Section 3.2). So from No we get:

> **Low**. *S* has a low degree of conviction that *p* at *t*.

Clearly, we cannot identify degrees of conviction with degrees of confidence if Low and High are jointly possible.

Further problems arise for Conviction–Confidence Identity because we can go lower than Low. For it's a logical, and surely a metaphysical, possibility that one can have an *extreme* disposition to rely *always and only* on the proposition *that p is very probable*. That is, one's disposition is so extreme that in *no* relevant world does one rely on *p*; rather, in relevant worlds one relies only on the proposition *that p is very probable*. According to DoC, one would count

[48] For discussion of the nature of credences see Eriksson and Hájek (2007), Clarke (2013), Buchak (2014), Greco (2015), Jackson (2020a,2020b), Moon and Jackson (2020), and Clarke & Staffel (2023).

as being not at all convinced, that is, having no degree of conviction. But even so, one might well have a very high confidence in p if, for example, they have a high degree of conviction that p is very probable. So not only is a high confidence in p compatible with a low degree of conviction in p, high confidence in p is also compatible with *no* degree of conviction in p.[49]

Section 2.3 noted the widespread view that standard lottery cases are cases where it is rational to be highly confident (L) *that one's ticket is a loser*, but it's not rational to believe it. If it's not rational to believe L, then it's not rational to have a degree of conviction in L sufficient for believing L is true. So one's rational degree of conviction must be reasonably low. So lottery cases are a kind of case where High and Low are rational. A surprising implication of this is that *degrees of conviction do not appear fit to be modelled probabilistically*, for if one's rational degrees of conviction are probabilistically coherent, then they do not violate the rule of negation: $\Pr(\neg p) = 1 - \Pr(p)$. But for one's degrees of conviction to obey this, one's low degree of conviction in L would require a correspondingly high degree of conviction in ¬L, that is, that one's ticket is *a winner*. But it's absurd to think that in a standard lottery case it is rational to have a high degree of conviction that one's lottery ticket is a winner. This suggests that even for ideal agents degrees of conviction are not required to be probabilistically coherent.[50]

But what of identifying our outright doxastic states with a maximal degree of confidence? The leading idea here involves identifying outright belief with maximum confidence ('credence 1') *in a context*, where one has maximum confidence in p in a context c just in case one relies on p in assertion, action, or deliberation in c in a way that does not take the possibility of $\neg p$ into account. The role of the contextual parameter, c, is to make sense of the fact that agents often seem to lack maximum confidence in p given the wide range of nearby situations in which they would rely on p in a hedged or qualified way that actually takes the possibility of $\neg p$ into account.

Following Clarke (2013:10) and Greco (2015), we'll call this view **sensitivism.**[51] Greco (2015) nicely illustrates the mechanics of this approach:

> If you ask me what time it is, I'll look at the lower right corner of my computer monitor and report, without hesitation, that it's 9:55 AM. That it's 9:55 seems like a pretty good candidate for something I (strongly) believe.

[49] For related thoughts see Williamson (2000:99) and Schulz (2021a,2021b) on degrees of 'outright belief'.

[50] For references concerning ranking theory as an alternative logic for rational degrees of conviction, see Schulz (2021b:8086–9) on the logic of degrees of 'outright belief'.

[51] For defence see Clarke (2013) and Greco (2015). However, see Greco (2015:97fn22) for a qualification and Greco (2023:ch.3) for additional contextualist resources for thinking about belief and fragmentation.

> But now suppose you ask me if I'm willing to bet my life that it's 9:55 for the chance to win a penny. Even while I continue to look at the monitor, which continues to display 9:55, I will demur. I'll allow that the computer might be wrong – perhaps it's a bit fast, or slow, or failed to update for daylight savings time, etc. If we rationally reconstruct my choice in decision theoretic terms, I'm clearly not treating the proposition that it's 9:55 as if it has probability 1. . . . what one believes may change in response to whether one has been offered [a bet]. In particular, one believes that it's 9:55 before being offered the bet – and thus, has credence 1 that it's 9:55 – but afterwards, one doesn't [believe it]. (Greco 2015:186)

There are problems with sensitivism. First, belief is an *unmasked* state according to sensitivism, that is, a state wherein one *relies on p* in *c*. But if the belief that *p* is a dispositional state (Section 4), then it can exist in cases where the agent doesn't rely on *p* (Section 6.2). If that's correct, then sensitivism's identification of belief with maximum confidence in context cannot be right. Second, it is generally counterintuitive to regard someone as *believing p* if it is only in a very narrow set of circumstances where one treats *p* as true. Suppose one were willing to assert and act on the claim that 2+2=4 only on Tuesdays at 9:55 am during leap years. It would be counterintuitive to claim that such a person believes 2+2=4. But one will have maximum confidence in context on just those occasions.[52]

We can build on this point in light of plausible practical-historical considerations. Plausibly, attention to the likely function and usefulness of our concepts can help illuminate their application conditions.[53] So take the following question: what function might outright doxastic concepts have served that can explain why these concepts were developed and passed on in human communities? One answer to this question stems from the plausible idea that the mental states we categorize as 'beliefs' are of obvious practical value to individuals themselves. As Crane (2013:164) has pointed out: *fleeting states* wherein one treats *p* as true are not to be categorized as beliefs because 'it is essential to beliefs that they persist through changes in current consciousness. Beliefs are stored in memory and can be called upon when future action is needed. It is crucial that they do this if they are to guide the actions of organisms in the way they do.' Leitgeb (2017:72–3) concurs: 'in order for belief to play its characteristic functional role in [decision-making, reasoning, and asserting] it needs to be sufficiently stable in the course of processes such as perception, supposition, and communication.' But sensitivism entails that considerations of stability and usefulness in future contexts have nothing to do with whether one believes *p* at *t*. So if this is right, there is

[52] See Frankish (2009:86), Crane (2013:165–6), Leitgeb (2017:70–4), and Wedgwood (2023:145).
[53] See Hannon (2019) for references and discussion.

a disconnect between the function belief fulfils for individuals and the function that can be fulfilled by maximum confidence in a context.

Another answer to the question in the previous paragraph concerns the role our outright states play in social coordination. It's quite plausible that part of what makes knowing about *other peoples'* outright doxastic states useful for us is that such information tells us something about how other people are disposed to respond in various situations. If I know that you are convinced that *p* but less than certain that *p*, then I know that while you're very likely to rely on *p* across a wide range of situations there will be some situations in which you will not rely on *p*. Knowing this about you is plainly valuable for coordinating behaviour and rational planning. But suppose I only know that you are willing to assert and act on the claim that 2+2=4 only on Tuesdays at 9:55 am during leap years. While that can be valuable information to have about you, it would be much more valuable for me to know what your reliance-dispositions are across a much wider range of situations. We would suggest that part of the practical value of knowing about people's outright doxastic states is that such information helps us successfully predict action and coordinate activities across *a reasonably wide range of different circumstances*. Knowing about people's beliefs, thinkings, convictions, and certainties clearly gives us *that* kind of information. But maximum confidence *in context* doesn't. So it seems problematic, or at least surprising, that our ordinary outright doxastic notions of believing, thinking, and conviction could be identical to such highly specific and fleeting states like maximum confidence in context.

Some have noted that sensitivism lacks the ability to account for the difference between belief and certainty and have suggested that fixing this requires attention to their modal profiles.[54] This abstract recommendation to 'go modal' is clearly in sync with BMW (Section 4.2). But notice that we need not only to *distinguish* belief from certainty, but also to distinguish thinking, conviction, and certainty in a way that enables us to explain T1–T8 (Section 2.2). It should be clear that sensitivism doesn't, as currently spelled out, have the ability to distinguish all these states in an explanatorily satisfactory way.[55]

[54] See Staffel's contribution in Clarke and Staffel (2023).

[55] The distinction between degrees of conviction and degrees of confidence is not clearly the same as Wedgwood's (2023) distinction between practical and theoretical degrees of confidence. In his own words:

> an agent's belief-system can only be adequately represented by two systems of credences . . . *theoretical credences* represent the way in which the agent registers, or keeps track of, the amount of justification that she has in favour of the relevant propositions, while *practical credences* are the credences on the basis of which the agent maintains and revises her intentions about how to act. (Wedgwood 2023:138)

We want to highlight that our criticisms of sensitivism are quite modest. Maximum confidence in context is definitely a condition that's worth calling a 'belief' in a stipulative sense. After all, maximum confidence in context is belief-like, and so when providing a Bayesian model of an agent's attitudes in a context it may well be optimal to model their outright states with subjective probability 1 in a context, for having a maximum confidence in p in a context c ensures that there is *at least some small proportion* of relevant worlds where one relies on p. So having maximum confidence in a context entails a non-zero degree of conviction according to DoC. But that non-zero degree of conviction does not entail that one has a disposition to rely on p that is strong enough for any of the outright states yet discussed, for all these states require reliance on p in a *sufficiently large* proportion of worlds, something that maximum confidence in a context doesn't alone ensure.

5.2 Degrees of Conviction Are Not Degrees of Phenomenal Conviction

Smithies (2023) argues that belief just is *the feeling of conviction* and that we can get a grip on this concept by considering the distinctive phenomenology associated with the gradual movement from the 'feeling of doubt' to the 'feeling of confidence' and finally towards a 'feeling of conviction'. Notice that the associated property here is a *phenomenal* (experiential) one.

Recall that Minimal Nature and DoC were motivated by the widely shared dispositional view of belief that connects belief to reliance-dispositions. The result was that degrees of conviction are degreed reliance-dispositions that are fit to be modelled quantitatively as a proportion across a set of worlds. And degrees of conviction in this sense can exist *whether or not* one's reliance-dispositions are accompanied by the phenomenal state indicated by Smithies. Indeed, the presence of a very strong feeling of conviction *does not* guarantee the presence of an outright state of conviction in the dispositional sense that we and many others think is central to our outright doxastic states. We would, of course, happily grant a contingent link between the two. But just as it's possible to have phenomenal visual experiences without being visually related to material objects in the world (visual hallucinations), it's possible to have strong feelings of conviction *in the absence of* the needed reliance-dispositions. In our view, the feeling of conviction without the associated reliance-dispositions strikes us as odd. *We* certainly would not classify someone as being convinced that p to any noteworthy degree unless they also had a reasonably strong disposition to rely on p.

However, we welcome a Chalmers-style reconciliation here. Chalmers (1996:16–23) argues that many mental state terms have both a phenomenal aspect and a psychological-functional aspect. And while in many typical instances the two aspects travel together, they can sometimes come apart. In the case of conviction, we think Smithies gives us a phenomenal state that typically travels with the psychological-functional state we've characterized. And we would suggest that Smithies has correspondingly given a theory of the phenomenal aspect of belief, not the functional aspect that we've sought to characterize and that seems to us fundamental to understanding *the practical value*[56] of conviction and other doxastic states.[57]

5.3 Degrees of Conviction Are Not Degrees of Revisability

Harman (1986:22) takes belief to be an on-off state and treats degrees of belief as degrees of difficulty associated with revising them. Could degrees of conviction likewise be identified with the ease/difficulty of revising an on-off state of conviction? No. First, a degree of conviction is the strength of one's disposition, and this is not the same kind of degreed property. The degree to which one is disposed to rely on *p* might be very low, but also very difficult to dislodge. Conversely, the degree to which one is disposed to rely on *p* might be very high, and yet very easy to dislodge. This is because dispositions can come and go more or less easily depending on the situation: a very sturdy glass can easily be made fragile if there is a diamond blade to hand, while a fragile glass might be virtually impossible to repair given the resources to hand.

So if one's degree of conviction in *p* is the strength of one's disposition to rely on *p*, then the ease/difficulty of revision is distinct from the weakness/strength of conviction. For strength of conviction is dispositional strength – and can be measured as a proportion across a set of worlds – and dispositional strength is not identical to how easy or hard it would be to remove the disposition or change that disposition. However, we should note that there can sometimes be a contingent link between the two: if one has a high degree of conviction that *p* because they have a lot of evidence in favour of *p*, it might be very hard to revise that degree of conviction because one has such strong evidence and because getting sufficient counter evidence will be challenging. But this is a contingent matter.[58]

[56] Something we discussed in Section 5.1 in connection with credence-1 sensitivism.

[57] See Leitgeb (2017:70–2) for references to a related historical discussion of this issue in Hume studies.

[58] See Frankish (2009) and Wedgwood (2023) for critical discussion of Harman's view. For a related discussion of resiliency see Skyrms (2011).

5.4 What Are Degrees of Belief?

We began Section 4 noting that belief is plausibly to be identified with either thinking, conviction, or assent, that is, B=A, or B=C, or B=T. Whatever view you prefer, so long as belief is taken to be a constitutively dispositional state (as indicated by Minimal Nature) and dispositions come in degrees, a natural idea would be to argue that degrees of belief just are dispositions to rely on *p* that vary in strength. For this reason there is some pressure to identify degrees of belief with degrees of conviction.

However, there is also contrary pressure. For it is extremely common to find epistemologists using the term 'degrees of belief' to refer to degrees of confidence. The fact that the expression 'degrees of belief' is so widely taken to refer to degrees of confidence suggests that we shouldn't pick a fight here about what kind of state the expression 'degrees of belief' refers to. When a theorist explicitly uses 'degrees of belief' to refer to degrees of confidence, that is what 'degrees of belief' *stipulatively* refers to in that authorial context. When this kind of stipulative use of the expression 'degrees of belief' occurs widely enough, the term 'degrees of belief' likely becomes polysemous.

But at this point in our inquiry this should not seem problematic, for we now have enough theory on the table that there need no longer be confusions about what one means with 'degree of belief' talk. A theorist can just come out and say that they're talking about degrees of conviction, or degrees of confidence, maximum confidence in context, degrees of phenomenal confidence, degrees of phenomenal conviction, degrees of revisability, or something else. So our view of the expression 'degrees of belief' is ecumenical and we begrudge none for using it. We ask only for a bit of descriptive clarity as 'degrees of belief' can be taken to refer to so many different degreed states.

6 Belief-Suspension Compatibilism

Sections 4 and 5 explored some of the consequences of the idea that our outright doxastic states – thinking, conviction, certainty, and belief – are constitutively dispositional states. This section further explores the consequences of this in regard to suspension. It is generally assumed that hosting an outright doxastic state, *D*, is incompatible with suspending *D*. For example, one cannot believe that *p* while being in a settled state wherein one suspends belief in *p*. But this is mistaken. There is a species of suspension, *non-interrogative suspension*, wherein one hosts an outright doxastic state *D* towards *p* while also *suspending the manifestations of that state*. An implication of this is that there exists a settled mental state that is constituted by an agent masking her belief that *p* from a disposition to do just that. We will call this *believing suspension.* Noting the existence of such states not only improves our theory of mind but it also provides new options for addressing old problems in epistemology.

6.1 Incompatibilism and the Species of Suspension

We will limit our discussion to the suspension of *belief.* But the lessons in this section hold for thinking, conviction, and even to some states of certainty. Among philosophers it is conventional to treat *belief* and the *suspension of belief* as incompatible mental states. Expressions of this are not hard to find:

> in suspending we do not attempt to believe truly, or to know. Indeed, suspension is a kind of non-believing, a not settling on an answer to the question of whether *p*. (Miracchi 2019:428)

> suspending is comprised of absences: the absence of affirming/believing and the absence of denying/disbelieving. (Sosa 2019:366)

> we can say without qualification that belief excludes suspending and refraining from belief. . . . these are success notions: if you suspend X, you don't X, and similarly for refraining. (McGrath 2021a:470)

We will capture this common[59] incompatibilist idea in with the following thesis:

Belief-Suspension Incompatibilism (BSI). It is impossible for any agent to suspend their belief that *p* while having the belief that *p* (relative to a single doxastic fragment[60] and without referential opacity[61]).

When it comes to states of suspension it is natural to take the proper objects of suspension to be *questions*: suspending *belief on whether p*, or suspending *on whether or not to believe p*, or suspending *on some more specific question.* When suspension does involve an interrogative complement it seems to imply *neutrality* on the answer to the referenced question. For example, if you have suspended belief *about whether* the phone was stolen, then you are in some way 'neutral' in regard to what the answer to

[59] Wedgwood (2002:272), Lord (2020:128), Raleigh (2021:2457), and Zinke (2021:1053).

[60] If our total set of doxastic states is fragmented into proper subsets of doxastic states (Borgoni et al. 2021), then thinkers might have distinct doxastic fragments wherein one might believe that *p* relative to one doxastic fragment, believe $\neg p$ relative to another doxastic fragment, *and also* suspend on whether *p* relative to yet another doxastic fragment. See Friedman (2017:305,322).

[61] On Millian/Russellian views of names, 'Clark Kent can fly' and 'Superman can fly' express the same proposition. But one can suspend belief on the latter while believing the former, owing to referential opacity and the guise under which one entertains the proposition. For discussions see Friedman (2017:322) and Atkins (2017).

that question is.[62] Let's use the term **suspension-wh** to refer to suspension relations that have questions as content and are connected in some way to indecision or neutrality.

If it only made sense to understand 'suspending belief' in terms of suspension-wh, then it might be a semantic error to talk of one *suspending their existing belief that p*. Since 'one's existing belief that *p*' does not have a question about whether *p* as content nor is one neutral about whether *p*. So something like BSI threatens to pop-out as a conceptual truth.[63]

But natural language does not limit suspension relations to suspension-wh. There is a wide range of uses of the term 'suspension' that do not require interrogative complements. Take the following:

(S1) The police department *suspended* the accused police officer *from* duty.
(S1′) *Die Polizeibehörde suspendierte den beschuldigten Polizeibeamten vom Dienst.*

(S2) The disciplinary committee *suspended* the rowdy students *from* attending university this week.
(S2′) *Der Disziplinarausschuss suspendierte die randalierenden Studenten für diese Woche vom Besuch der Universität.*

The sense of 'suspension' here lacks interrogatives and lacks reference to a question. It also lacks implications about agential neutrality. Structurally, these suspension relations have the following form: where *x* and *y* stand for individuals and *F* stands for some predicate:

Minimal Structure. *x* suspended *y* from *F-ing (/being F).*

Let's use the term **suspension-from** to refer to suspension relations that are referenced with expressions that conform to Minimal Structure. We cannot reduce suspension-from to suspension-wh: suspension-wh requires a question as an object, suspension-from does not.

Strikingly, it seems possible to reduce suspension-wh to a kind of suspension-from. To see why, observe that suspension-wh expressions can be rewritten as suspension-from expressions:

(S3) She suspends belief **about whether** it's raining.
(S3′) *Sie hält eine Überzeugung darüber zurück, ob es regnet.*[64]

---

[62] Sturgeon (2010), Friedman (2017), Miracchi (2019), Sosa (2019), Staffel (2019), Lord (2020), McGrath (2021a), Raleigh (2021), and Wagner (2022).

[63] Lord (2020), McGrath (2021a:470), and Wagner (2022:690).

[64] This translation calls for two clarifications. First, our translation of 'belief' as '*Überzeugung*' is not intended as a philosophical statement about the nature of belief. In Section 6.2 we provided reasons to

(S4) She suspends **herself** from holding (forming or sustaining) a belief about whether it's raining.

(S4′) *Sie hält sich davon zurück, eine Überzeugung darüber zu haben (formen oder behalten), ob es regnet.*

(S4) feels clunky and verbose, but not ungrammatical or meaningless. The same goes for (S4′).

Is (S4)'s meaning different from the meaning of (S3)? Some might feel like (S4) entails a degree of attention, intentional activity, or conscious exercise of one's personal agency that (S3) lacks. But that's a pragmatic implicature, not a semantic entailment. To see this, consider a deadman's brake. Its function is to halt the motion of a vehicle if its operator is absent or incapacitated. Now consider a particular vehicle with such a brake: it's a vehicle that can *suspend itself from moving* even though it lacks the capacity for attention, intentional activity, or a conscious exercise of personal agency. Even when we turn our attention to mature humans, while paradigmatic cases where one suspends belief involve a conscious exercise of personal agency, there can also be cases where an agent's *sub-personal cognitive processes* bring an agent to suspend themselves from holding a belief effortlessly and without conscious attention. Since so many of our processes of belief-revision are automatic, effortless, and not in need of conscious attention, this point should be unproblematic.

Once implicatures connected to conscious and intentional agency are set aside, we detect no semantic difference between (S3) and (S4). At the very least, they appear to be logically equivalent: (S3) entails (S4), and vice versa. To see this, suppose they were not logically equivalent. Then at least one of the following states should be logically possible:

(S3 & ¬S4) She suspended belief about whether it's raining, but she did not suspend herself from holding (forming or sustaining) a belief about whether it's raining.

identify 'belief' with '*Fürwahrhalten*', and we stand by that. Rather, the translation reflects the fact that '*Fürwahrhalten*' as well as '*Glaube*' – which is another popular translation of 'belief' – both seem to resist the German interrogative '*darüber, ob*', whereas '*Überzeugung*' doesn't. Second, we had previously translated 'suspend' as '*suspendieren*' (see (S1) and (S2)), but now opt for '*zurückhalten*'. This shift simply reflects the fact that the contemporary German term '*suspendieren*' isn't as permissive as the English term 'suspend' – nowadays, '*suspendieren*' is mostly used in contexts where one is suspended from a role. Moreover, '*zurückhalten*' has the added advantage of explicating the sense of 'suspend' as 'putting off', which we will rely on later. We believe, however, that both German terms express the same underlying concept of suspension-from. With that being said, we find historical precedent for a broader use of the German term '*suspendieren*' in Kant. For example, Kant writes: 'Sein Urtheil nach Maximen *zu suspendieren*, dazu wird eine geübte Urtheilskraft erfordert' (9:74; our emphasis). For similar uses of '*suspendieren*' in Kant, see (9:84), (24:211–2,555,557,640,885). Thus, although it sounds strange to twenty-first-century German ears, it may not be ungrammatical to say '*S* suspendieret die Überzeugung (hinsichtlich der Frage) darüber, ob *p*'.

(S3′ & ¬S4′) *Sie hält eine Überzeugung darüber zurück, ob es regnet, aber sie hält sich nicht davon zurück, eine Überzeugung darüber zu haben (formen oder behalten), ob es regnet.*

(S4 & ¬S3) She suspended herself from holding (forming or sustaining) a belief about whether it's raining, but she did not suspend belief about whether it's raining.

(S4′ & ¬S3′) *Sie hält sich davon zurück, eine Überzeugung darüber zu haben (formen oder behalten), ob es regnet, aber sie hält nicht eine Überzeugung darüber zurück, ob es regnet.*

Both strike us as confusing as thoughts about married bachelors. To our ears, this is owed purely to the semantic content of the constitutive claims.

Suspension-from expressions are also connected to what McGrath (2021b) takes to be the core concept of suspension. The *Oxford English Dictionary*'s first category of senses for 'suspend' connect it to debarring, postponing, and deferring. McGrath calls this the 'putting-off' or 'waiting' sense of suspension. His view that the putting-off sense of suspension is primary is supported by the examples given earlier in this section where suspension expressions satisfy Minimal Structure. For example, to suspend a police officer from duty is to *suspend* them *from* being able to lawfully enforce the law, that is, to *put off* their ability to do just that. To *suspend* a student *from* attending university is to *put off* their ability to properly take advantage of the right university students have to attend university. To *suspend* a campaign *from* continuing or from beginning until later is to *put off* its continuance or beginning. We'll argue in the following sections that one can suspend a belief by, what one could describe as, 'putting off' the manifestation of one's belief.

6.2 Masking a Belief's Dispositions

To understand how belief is compatible with the suspension of belief, it helps to consider the nature of dispositions and masks. *Fragility* can be analysed as having a disposition to break when struck. Familiar character traits are also treated as dispositions: to be *irascible* is to have a disposition to be angered when provoked. In these examples, being struck and being provoked are stimulus conditions for their respective dispositions: they are conditions that trigger the characteristic manifestations of these dispositions (breaking, becoming angry).

As is well known, dispositions can be masked. Masks obstruct the manifestation of an object's disposition without undermining the object's possession of the disposition or the obtaining of the disposition's stimulus condition. Fragile glasses wrapped in packing material retain their disposition to break when struck even if they survive being struck due to the packing material; an ingested poison has a disposition to induce illness when swallowed even if one has simultaneously taken an antidote that prevents illness. In such cases, the stimulus of the disposition is present (a striking, a swallowing) though the disposition fails to manifest (no breaking, no illness) due to a mask (packing material, antidotes).[65]

Discussions of masking have typically focused on *extrinsic* masks, that is, sources that bring about the masking of an object's disposition that are not intrinsic to the object in question. But the sources that cause masking need not be extrinsic. Intrinsic masking is a special case of masking that occurs when an object has a disposition to mask the manifestation *of its own* dispositions when the relevant stimulus condition obtains. We will call this **self-masking**. We are, for instance, disposed to feel outrage *and display offence* at certain jokes; however, we can be disposed to refrain from displaying offence when offended in the special case where displaying offence might cost our job. When this happens we mask our disposition to display offence from a disposition to do so. For another example, many of us are disposed to move away from people who approach us with needles. But when we recognize that we're in a medical situation where it has become clear that we need a shot and when we recognize that it's a medical professional approaching us, we mask this disposition: we choose to remain in place and accept being poked with a needle. But in nearly all other situations where we are approached with needles we move away.

These examples are cases of **partial self-masking**, for they are cases where we have a disposition to mask another disposition in *only some* of the situations where its stimulus condition obtains. For example, in the strong majority of cases where we're approached with needles we do not mask our disposition to move away, as being stuck with a needle hurts and there are all kinds of risks associated with being stuck with a needle by non-medical professionals in non-medical contexts.

Structurally, partial self-masking is a matter of an object having the following dispositions:

(D1) x has a disposition to F when c.
(PSM) x has a disposition to itself bring it about that x does not-F when $c\&c^*$ obtain, where $c \neq c^*$.

The possibility of partial self-masking, so defined, is neatly accommodated by the Dispositional Proportionality Principle.[66] Recall that in this view: x is

[65] Johnston (1992:233–4), Manley and Wasserman (2007, 2008, 2011), Everett (2009), Ashwell (2010), and Vetter (2015).

[66] In contrast to partial self-masking, there is a concept of *total self-masking*, which would involve an object, x, having the two following dispositions: x has a disposition to F ***when c***, and x has a disposition to mask that disposition ***when c***. Usually, it is *total* (not merely *partial*) self-masking

disposed to F if and only if x Fs in *a sufficiently high proportion* of the relevant worlds where its stimulus condition obtains (see Section 4.2). In such a view, simultaneously satisfying D1 and PSM can be modelled with Figure 4.

Since the $c\&c^*$-worlds are a small subset of the c-worlds, it is possible for there to be enough c-worlds where x Fs for x to have the disposition to F when c. And since x does not-F in nearly all the $c\&c^*$-worlds it is possible for x to have a disposition to bring it about that it does not-F in $c\&c^*$. So when x is in a $c\&c^*$-world on the inside of the $\neg F$ line, x's disposition to F when c is masked. So not only is the possibility of having a self-masking disposition consistent with the Dispositional Proportionality Principle, it is a possibility that appears to be entailed by it.

What have self-masking dispositions to do with suspension? Recall our toy instance of Minimal Nature: MAD. MAD says you believe that p only if you're disposed to rely on p in assertion, action, or deliberation when you take p to be relevant (Section 4.1). If MAD is true, then the metaphysics of belief entail that beliefs can be masked. To see how you might partially self-mask your own beliefs, consider the following scenario:

> **Disagreement**. You and a friend are about to split the bill for dinner via mental math. You do your mental math, dividing the bill by two, and you come up with €43.82. You triple check your math, you get the same answer each time. So (i) you come to hold the belief that you owe exactly €43.82, that is, you come to have a disposition to assert, act on, and deliberate on that claim when you take it to be relevant. (ii) You have a standing disposition to mask (rather than eliminate) your disposition in (i) when you learn of

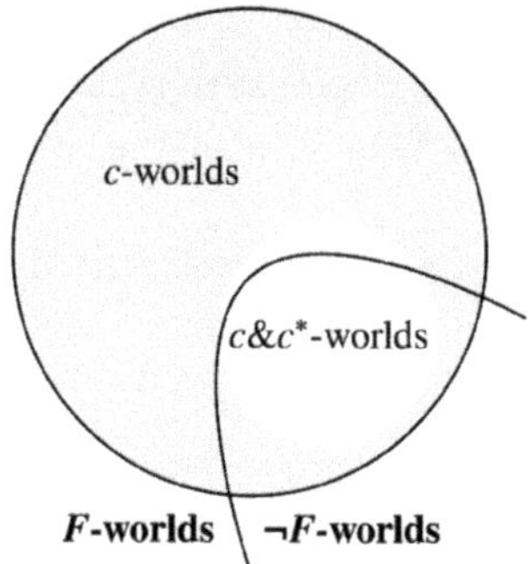

Figure 4 Partial self-masking.

that concerns those who debate whether an object can have a disposition to mask manifestations of its own dispositions. For defence of total self-masks (intrinsic masks) see Everett (2009), Ashwell (2010), Clarke (2010), and Kittle (2015). For opposition, see Handfield (2008) and Choi (2013,2017).

a disagreeing peer. And (iii) you come to learn of a disagreeing peer when you share your answer with your friend who claims that you both owe €43.84, not €43.82. Because of this you mask your belief's dispositions.[67]

To see how partial self-masking can happen in a case like this we need to look at the relevant possibility space. First, situations like Disagreement can have different kinds of stakes apparently associated with them, and you might mask your belief *only under some* apparent stakes conditions. For example:

1. One might be in an apparent *false-belief high-stakes* situation. That is, you take yourself to be in a case where: if you believe *p* and you're wrong, then relying on *p* might bring about (or introduce a high risk of) some very bad outcome.
2. One might be in an apparent *false-belief medium-stakes* situation. That is, you take yourself to be in a case where: if you believe *p* and you're wrong, then relying on *p* might bring about (or introduce a high risk of) some mildly bad outcome.
3. One might be in an apparent *false-belief low-stakes* situation. That is, you take yourself to be in a case where: there is little-to-no penalty if you're wrong about *p*.
4. One might be in an apparent *true-belief high-stakes* situation. That is, you take yourself to be in a case where: if you're right about *p* and *you don't rely on it*, you risk some seriously bad outcome.
5. One might be in an apparent *true-belief medium-stakes* situation. That is, you take yourself to be in a case where: if you're right about *p* and *you don't rely on it*, you risk some mildly bad outcome.
6. One might be in an apparent *true-belief low-stakes* situation. That is, you take yourself to be in a case where: if you're right about *p* and you *don't rely on it*, there is no risk of a bad outcome.

Second, one can be in different kinds of inquiry settings:

7. One thinks that further inquiry is easy/possible with the available time and resources.
8. One thinks that further inquiry may be hard/impossible with the available time and resources.
9. One thinks that further inquiry/double-checking is required along at least one normative dimension (moral, practical, epistemic).
10. One thinks that further inquiry/double-checking is best, whether or not it is required.

[67] Recall in Section 4.2 that belief's dispositions were characterized in terms of worlds where one's apparent evidence supports *p* to a sufficient extent. In cases of disagreement, so long as one doesn't take the fact of peer disagreement itself to indicate $\neg p$, then this condition on belief can be satisfied.

Third, one can be in different kinds of higher-order evidential settings:

11. One can have apparently *strong first-order evidence for p* and *weak negative higher-order evidence*. For example, in Disagreement one's negative higher-order evidence to think they made a mistake (stemming from the peer disagreement) can be weakened due to evidence that one's peer might be trying to play a joke or failed to double-check their mental math.
12. One can have apparently *strong first-order evidence for p* and *strong negative higher-order evidence*.

These conditions are fairly coarse-grained and can be combined in various ways, leading to far more than twelve types of possibilities in which the case Disagreement might be realized.

Now, to see *one way* in which partial self-masking might occur in a way that leads to believing that *p* while also masking that belief, take an agent in a case like Disagreement who believes that *p* and their dispositional profile satisfies the following conditions:

> **Masking Condition**. *S* has a disposition to mask her belief that *p* when *p* is taken to be relevant if: either (i) her negative high-order evidence is strong and not significantly undermined by further available evidence, or (ii) she is in a false-belief high-stakes situation.

> **Non-Masking Condition**. *S* lacks a disposition to mask her belief that *p* when *p* is taken to be relevant if any condition other than (i) or (ii) above obtain.

If one satisfies these conditions, then, *ceteris paribus*, there is a much greater proportion of cases in which one manifests rather than masks one's dispositions; after all, one masks one's belief *in only two* of the twelve plus kinds of cases sketched here. So if an agent is in one of those two masking conditions and one's dispositional profile fits these conditions, then one will satisfy the conditions for being in a state of belief in *p* (because they have a disposition to rely on *p*), but also as having a triggered disposition to mask that belief state. While these cursory thoughts inspire further questions, they also establish a burden of proof on those who would deny that beliefs can be partially self-masked from a disposition to do so.

6.3 Belief-Suspension Compatibilism

What should we say of someone who has a *disposition to display offence when offended* in circumstances where she masks that disposition from another disposition to do just that? What is *the status* of the masked disposition? Since she masks her disposition to display offence when offended in such circumstances, the manifestation of her disposition is *put off*. Put differently, the reliance-dispositions constitutive of one's belief are *suspended from manifesting*.

Let's provide a general characterization of the conditions under which belief's reliance-dispositions can be suspended that would fit the phenomenon of self-masking we have observed in the previous section:

> **Sufficient for Suspending Belief**. Necessarily, *S* suspends her belief that *p* **if**:
>
> (i) *S* believes *p*, and thus *S* has the reliance-dispositions constitutive of belief (e.g., in regard to assertion, action, and deliberation when taking *p* to be relevant), and
>
> (ii) *S* has a disposition to mask her dispositions in (i) when taking *p* to be relevant under some conditions *c**, and
>
> (iii) *S* manifests her disposition in (ii).

This is a mere sufficient condition since we want to leave room for cases where one suspends belief *on whether p*, that is, instances of suspension-wh discussed in Section 6.1.

Given the observations of the previous section it is easy to construct cases involving an existing belief where (i)–(iii) obtain. Indeed, we've seen it with the case labelled 'Disagreement'. In that case, Disagreement(i) implies that you believe that you owe exactly €43.82. And since Sufficient for Suspending Belief(i)–(iii) are satisfied in Disagreement(i)–(iii), it follows that you have suspended your belief that you owe exactly €43.82. So any case where Disagreement(i)–(iii) holds is a case where you believe that you owe exactly €43.82 and have also suspended that belief. *This is inconsistent with BSI*. So if Sufficient for Suspending Belief is true, it follows that BSI is false.

Let's use the term **believing suspension** to refer to suspended belief states that are suspended owing to satisfying Sufficient for Suspending Belief(i)–(iii). We can characterize such states as follows:

> **Believing Suspension**: *S believingly suspends* on $p =_{\text{df}}$
>
> (i) *S* believes that *p* (and thus has the reliance-dispositions constitutive of believing that *p*), and
>
> (ii) *S* has a disposition to mask her belief that *p* under some conditions *c**, and
>
> (iii) *S* manifests her disposition in (ii).

Condition (iii) is crucial for two reasons. First, believing suspension is a state wherein an agent *has actually suspended her belief from manifesting*. But an agent can have *a disposition to do that* without actually suspending her belief. For example, you can have a disposition to suspend your belief that *p* from manifesting in response to peer disagreement *without being in a case of disagreement*. It's only *after* learning that you're in a case of peer disagreement that your disposition to mask is triggered and you suspend your belief that *p* by masking it.

The second reason condition (iii) is important is that we can, and should, distinguish between suspensions of belief *that are doxastic states of an agent* from those that are not. For a belief (or any disposition) to be suspended via masking it need only be the case that it be prevented from manifesting when its stimulus condition obtains. But this can happen without being caused by any set of dispositions that stem from *within the agent* herself, as one can imagine all manner of possible interventions from external factors. If believing suspension is to be a genuine doxastic state *of the believer*, then the source of the suspension of her belief must lie within the believer and stem from a disposition that she has to mask her belief. This is what condition (iii) ensures and this is what makes it plausible to claim that believing suspension is a genuine doxastic state of the agent herself.

We have in this section focused on belief. But we also have thinking, conviction, and certainty. This raises a question: can every outright doxastic state be suspended via self-masking? No. There is a limit involving states of certainty. Recall the Lewis–Unger debate summarized at the end of Section 4.2. There we indicated an attraction to Lewis's idea that we could be certain that *p* according to a less demanding standard of precision that allows for some proportion of worlds where we don't rely on *p*. But now we can see that there is at least one demanding sense of certainty to which we can apply Unger's uber-standard. Let us say that an agent *S* is *absolutely* certain that *p* just in case there is no relevant world (e.g., as specified by BSW) in which *S* takes *p* to be relevant and *S* stops herself from manifesting the reliance-dispositions constitutive of believing *p*.[68] Being absolutely certain is a way of believing, but not one that is susceptible to self-masking since it excludes all subregions *c** wherein the agent does not rely on *p*.

6.4 Consequences of Believing Suspension

Observing the existence of believing suspension clearly improves our theory of mind by drawing attention to different conditions our doxastic states might exist

[68] We can define an even more demanding concept of certainty that some people seem to have in mind when using the phrase 'absolute certainty'. Let us say that an agent is *immovably* absolutely certain that *p* if and only if she is absolutely certain that *p* and there is no psychologically possible world in which: she gets new information and she ceases to be absolutely certain that *p*. Compare Unger (1975).

in. Believing suspension also holds interesting implications for recent work in epistemology. To help you anticipate them, take a standard case of peer disagreement over whether *p*, like Disagreement from Section 6.2. Consider whether the following could jointly hold in such a case:

> **Conciliate**. You are required to suspend your belief that you owe *n* because your peer disagrees with you and you know that sometimes you make mistakes.[69]
>
> **Remain Steadfast (When Right)**. You are required to believe that you owe *n* because you correctly performed your mathematical calculations.[70]

If belief and the suspension of belief were incompatible states then the truth of these would entail that rationality requires us to do the impossible, thereby yielding a dilemma of rationality. However, we've seen that belief and the suspensions of manifestations of one's beliefs are compatible. So both can be true without yielding dilemmas of rationality.

An implication of this is that conciliatory and non-conciliatory views of peer disagreement are not logically incompatible. This observation merits a reassessment of the peer disagreement literature and the arguments that have structured that debate over the last two decades. This literature is too large to explore here in any meaningful way.[71] Our aim in this short section is just to help readers see the burgeoning new space of possibilities for addressing certain problems in epistemology that are structured around situations where normative recommendations to believe and to suspend belief appear to be in tension.

7 Was Kant a Kantian about Doxastic States? by Christopher Benzenberg

What might Kant have made of the Kantian Threshold View and its associated theses from Sections 2, 3, 4, 5, and 6? In this section, we argue that Kant not only inspires them, but that they also enjoy textual support. We proceed by reconstructing Kant's claims about the structural relations between thinking/opinion, conviction, and certainty; specifically, whether Kant would have (or at least could have) accepted T=O, T=SC, and T1–T8 (Section 7.1). Additionally, we consider which doxastic state in Kant's taxonomy of assent most closely corresponds to the present-day notion of belief, that is, Kant's view on B=T, B=C, and B=A (Section 7.2).

---

[69] Christensen (2007). [70] Kelly (2005) and Titelbaum (2015).

[71] Arguably, the connected puzzle of misleading higher-order evidence likewise seems in need of reassessment in light of believing suspension. See Silva (2016).

7.1 Kant on Opinion, Conviction, and Certainty

Kant, the historical person, may not have labelled himself a 'Kantian', in our sense of the term. Kant's theory of assent owes much to George Friedrich Meier's *Excerpt from the Doctrine of Reason* (1752), which served as the textbook for Kant's logic lectures. Meier, who discusses assent, opinion, conviction, and certainty extensively,[72] was himself influenced by Book IV of Locke's (1975/1690) *Essay Concerning Human Understanding.*[73] Indeed, Locke prominently discusses the notions of assent, opinion, and certainty;[74] yet, unlike Kant and Meier, Locke doesn't properly theorize conviction.[75] So rather than speculating about Kant's self-ascription, we should look at the letter of his text to determine whether Kant really was a Kantian.

Does Kant identify thinking and opinion (T=O)? Answer: It's left open by Kant's texts. Ordinary language draws no distinction between the states referred to by the expressions '*S* thinks that *p*' ('*S denkt, dass p*') and 'It is *S*'s opinion that *p*' ('*Es ist S' Meinung, dass p*'). But Kant draws a technical distinction. While opinion is introduced as a species of assent (A822/B850), thinking involves the unique, spontaneous activity of the understanding, or higher faculty of cognition in general (cf. A19/B33; A50/B74).

Understood in this broad sense, thinking is not a propositional attitude, but attaches to all our representations (*Vorstellungen*): 'The *I think* must be able to accompany all my *representations*; for otherwise something would be represented in me that could not be thought at all' (B131–2; our emphasis). Kant therefore does not limit his notion of thinking to the instances that involve a sentential complement, that is, 'thinks *that p*'. Rather, he allows for broader technical uses, like 'I think "table"', where the 'I think' accompanies my representation of a table. Since Kant doesn't discuss sententially complemented constructions like '*S* thinks that *p*', it is, strictly speaking, left open by the text what Kant would say about such constructions and how they relate to 'It is *S*'s opinion that *p*'.[76]

[72] See §168 for assent, §§181–3 for opinion, §§184–6 for conviction, and ch.I.6 for certainty.

[73] Kant would have read Heinrich Poley's German translation of Locke's *Essay* from 1757. Insole (2019) provides a helpful outline of the link between Locke, Meier, and Kant, focusing on their respective notions of belief, faith, and *Glaube*.

[74] References to Locke's *Essay* (E) are to the corresponding book, chapter, and section. Key passages on 'assent', which Locke contrasts with 'dissent', include E IV.xiv.3, E IV.xv.1–3, E IV.xvi.14. Locke discusses opinion in E IV.ii.14, E IV.iii.6, E IV.xv.3, and E IV.xvi.4. For Locke on certainty, see especially E IV.ii.1 and E IV.vi.3.

[75] While Locke, like Kant, admits 'degrees of assent', he specifies them as degrees of 'confidence' (E IV.xv.1). Conviction, by contrast, is only mentioned a handful of times (e.g., in E IV.i.9).

[76] That said, Kant's notion of thinking-in-general as spontaneous activity can be read as placing thinking-in-general outside the order of nature. If thinking-that just is opinion-that, Kant's stance on thinking-in-general may stand in tension with the account of thinking/opinion-that as a dispositional state. Moreover, thinking-in-general seems to involve a type of epistemic

Does Kant think that opinion is psychologically weaker than certainty and conviction (T1, T6)? Answer: Yes. But to see why, we first need to reintroduce some of the complexities of Kant's theory of assent that we bracketed in Section 2.1. Recall that Kant's full notion of opinion doesn't just denote a doxastic attitude (which we coined 'subjective opinion'), but a doxastic attitude whose strength is proportional to the evidence, or what Kant calls 'objective grounds' (A820/B848). And while 'subjective conviction' (A824/B852) and 'subjective certainty' (24:437) denote purely doxastic attitudes, they do have epistemic counterparts, which Kant calls 'logical conviction' (9:72) and 'logical certainty' (A829/B857); logical certainty roughly aligns with what many now call 'epistemic certainty'.[77]

Keeping in line with Kant's concept of opinion as a doxastic state whose strength is proportional to its evidential support, we suggest that the strength of subjective certainty and subjective conviction is proportional to the evidential support of logical certainty and logical conviction. This proportionality between degrees of evidential support and degrees of strength of the corresponding doxastic attitude ('doxastic strength', for short) has a major exegetical payoff that we leverage throughout this section.

Kant tends to focus his discussion on the epistemic profile of opinion, logical conviction, and logical certainty, while remaining tight-lipped about their corresponding doxastic strengths. Our primary aim, however, is to better understand the doxastic attitudes and their relative degrees of doxastic strength in Kant's theory. The proportionality claim thus allows us to draw inferences about Kant's largely implicit views on the degrees of doxastic strength from his explicit statements about degrees of evidential support associated with logical certainty, logical conviction, and opinion.

With that out of the way, let's get back to T1 and T6. Kant is clear that opinion requires weaker evidence or objective grounds than logical conviction and certainty. Logical conviction and certainty both require *sufficient* objective grounds (that license knowledge): 'objectively sufficient ... assent is called *conviction*' (A820/B848; our emphasis) and 'certainty is objective sufficiency of assent' (24:734).[78] Opinion, on the other hand, is defined as 'objectively

autonomy that opinion lacks; after all, Kant asks us 'to think for ourselves' (9:57), yet we are permitted to form opinions from the testimony of others (8:141).

[77] We suggest that 'logical conviction' tracks the sense of 'conviction' Kant uses in the first four paragraphs of Section 3 of the Canon (A820–1/B848–9); it is in this logical sense of conviction that Kant contrasts conviction with persuasion (*Überredung*) (A820–1/B848–9; see also Gava 2024). Note also that Kant has additional notions of 'moral conviction' (5:463) and 'moral certainty' (A829/B855). We bracket these moral notions from our discussion and focus on the relation between logical and subjective conviction and certainty.

[78] Just two pages later, Kant also states that the '*subjective* sufficiency is called conviction' (A822/B850; our emphasis). But there is no tension here if we distinguish between logical and subjective conviction.

insufficient assent' (A822/B850). Moreover, Kant measures the strength of objective grounds via an assent's (evidential) probability;[79] and while logical certainty serves as the 'yardstick' (9:82) of all degrees of probability, giving it probability 1, opinion requires only a probability of above 0.5.[80]

Opinion thus rests on weaker evidence than logical certainty and conviction. Since the doxastic strength constitutive of opinion is proportional to its evidence, Kant must also think that opinion is doxastically weaker than subjective certainty and conviction, and so accept T1 and T6. This conclusion is independently supported by Kant's claim that 'subjective conviction' is a 'firm' ('*festes*') assent, on which we would bet much of life's fortunes (A824–5/B852–3).[81] This point plausibly generalizes to subjective certainty, but not to opinion, which Kant thinks extends to 'preliminary judgements' ('*vorläufiges Urtheilen*') (9:66) and even mere suspicions (R2450, 16:373); and, surely, suspicion needn't be firm.

Could Kant have accepted that thinking/opinion is to be understood as being at least somewhat convinced (T=SC)? Answer: Yes. While Kant's discussion usually focuses on our *outright* attitudes, he occasionally talks about *degreed* attitudes, especially when discussing their epistemic profile. Most notably, Kant specifies that evidentially justified assent – that is, assent that rests on objective grounds – has a 'degree of probability' ('*Grad der Wahrscheinlichkeit*') (24:196). Now, remember that Kant's notion of probability serves as a measure of the strength of an assent's evidence/objective ground. Thus, an 'opinion' must have a 'degree of probability' (2:139) that indicates the strength of its objective ground.[82]

Probability isn't the only thing that comes in degrees. Since logical certainty, which rests on sufficient objective grounds, serves as the yardstick of all lower degrees of probability, Kant suggests that degrees of probability are effectively degrees of logical certainty – 'degree of certainty or probability' (28:6; see also 24:199).[83] We should therefore expect that opinion, which has a degree of

[79] In fact, Kant *defines* probability (*Wahrscheinlichkeit*) as the fraction of the objective ground we have over the sufficient objective ground (cf. R2452, 16:375, and 24:196). On this definition, all assent from sufficient objective grounds has probability 1.

[80] See (5:465), (9:82), and (24:241).

[81] While Kant sometimes seems to limit the betting touchstone to faith (cf. 6:305, R2450, 16:373–4), he also uses betting to test all assent that is subjectively sufficient, and so entails subjective conviction (cf. 9:73).

[82] Insofar as objective grounds track truth, Kant also talks about an assent's 'degree of truth' (24:143; see also 24:367). Of course, Kant doesn't mean to say that truth itself comes in degrees, but that the objective ground on which the probable assent rests is a degree of the sufficient ground, which entails truth (cf. R2595, 16:434; 24:884).

[83] In the *Critique of Judgement*, Kant suggests a mereological relation between degrees of probability and certainty: 'Probability is a part of . . . certainty' (5:465). There are many passages that more generally suggest that certainty can come in degrees. See, for example, (2:155), (R3707, 17:245), and (27:566, 1292).

probability (as we have seen), also has some degree of logical certainty. And indeed, when Kant examines the 'opinions' of different metaphysical schools, he notes in passing that they must have some 'degree of certainty' (2:275).

But what about degrees of conviction? Note first that Kant occasionally uses graded terms when talking about logical conviction. For example, he thinks that there can be 'greater conviction' (2:265) and even a 'greatest conviction' (1:458). Moreover, logical conviction, like logical certainty, rests on sufficient objective grounds, which is why degrees of probability are effectively also degrees of logical conviction. Kant should, therefore, have been able to specify opinion as having a degree of logical conviction that depends on the strength of its objective grounds. Now given the proportionality between evidential support and doxastic strength, these epistemic degrees should be mirrored on the doxastic level. So Kant could easily have understood the doxastic dimension of opinion in terms of being at least somewhat (subjectively) convinced.

Would Kant have endorsed that certainty and conviction both entail thinking/opinion (T2, T3)? Answer: Perhaps, once a clarification is made. As we have noted, Kant defines opinion as a state based on insufficient objective grounds (A822/B850). Logical certainty, on the other hand, requires sufficient objective grounds for assent (A822/B850), as does logical conviction (A820/B848). Thus understood, logical certainty and conviction would have to exclude opinion; after all, sufficient grounds aren't insufficient. Given the proportionality of evidence to doxastic strength, it would follow that subjective certainty and conviction would have to exclude opinion as well. Kant, thus, seems inclined to deny T2 and T3.

However, we think this would be a merely verbal dispute between us and Kant. For Kant's notion of 'opinion' maps onto what we would call *'mere* opinion', that is, opinion and nothing stronger than opinion. Indeed, Kant occasionally even specifies that he is talking about 'mere opinion' ('*bloße Meinung*') (20:61; see also 9:67). This leaves space for Kant to allow that certainty and conviction entail the absence of mere opinion, while also allowing that certainty and conviction entail the presence of non-mere opinion. Indeed, this would also explain why Kant, in the *Living Forces* essay (1747), refers to the 'opinions' of Descartes and Leibniz as 'convictions' (1:15). Kant, therefore, might have accepted T2 and T3 after all.

Is conviction psychologically weaker than certainty for Kant (T4, T8)? Answer: It's complicated. On the surface, Kant appears to identify logical conviction and logical certainty. Both, we have seen, require the same amount of evidential support – namely, sufficient objective grounds – and so logical certainty and logical conviction should entail each other. In the *Jäsche Logic*, Kant confirms one direction of this entailment: if 'we are logically convinced on objective grounds', then 'the object is certain' (9:72; see also A820–9/B848–57). What is true of logical certainty and logical conviction should also be true of their subjective counterparts. So if logical conviction and logical certainty are identical, then subjective conviction and subjective certainty should also be identical. Indeed, Kant seems to explicitly identify the two subjective states: 'conviction or subjective certainty' (R2695, 16:473). So, Kant seems to accept T4 but deny T8.

But the issue is more complicated. Let us consider a species of assent Kant calls 'pragmatic Belief' ('*pragmatischer Glaube*') (A824/B852) – the capital 'B' indicates that this is a technical term for Kant, not to be confused with our modern sense of 'belief'. While Kant's notion of pragmatic Belief is interesting for a number of reasons, it has two important characteristics that are important for us now: (i) Kant states that pragmatic Belief, like all species of Belief or faith (*Glaube*), involves 'subjective conviction' (824/B852); moreover, (ii) Kant also insists that pragmatic Belief need not be subjectively certain, because pragmatic Belief 'has only a degree' of conviction because we wouldn't bet the 'fortunes of the entire life' on its truth (A825/B853). Kant's account of pragmatic Belief, thus, puts textual pressure on the seeming identification of subjective conviction with subjective certainty.

And perhaps we can relieve this textual pressure. Kant occasionally seems to identify (or at least align) logical certainty with the highest degree of logical conviction. For example, he remarks: 'The grounds I have given . . . are not of the kind that provide the *greatest conviction and certainty*' (1:458; our emphasis). Elsewhere he states that 'the *certainty* of a mechanical doctrine of the origin of the universe . . . is the *highest peak of conviction*' (1:341; our emphasis). Based on such passages, we make the following proposal: whenever Kant identifies certainty with conviction – be it logical or subjective – he implicitly identifies certainty with the greatest conviction; outright conviction, by contrast, needn't constitute a state of subjective certainty. On this reading, then, Kant may have accepted T8 after all.[84]

Would Kant allow for cases where it is rational to think that p even if one knows that: while p is more likely than ¬p, ¬p is almost as likely as p (T5)? Answer: Yes. Kant frequently states that opinion merely requires 'more grounds for a cognition than against it', thereby making it more probable than its opposite (24:241).[85] All assent that is more probable than its opposite is also called probable *simpliciter* (9:81–2),[86] and so 'someone who adheres to an opinion holds the opinion to be

[84] See our discussion of 'sure' in footnote 21, as it provides a possible explanation for why Kant might have been of two minds here. For even though there's good philosophical reason to think 'conviction' and 'certainty' are separate, the potentially complicated relationship between 'conviction' and 'sure' could easily lead one to link conviction to certainty.

[85] See (R2450, 16:373), (R2480, 16:388), and (24:219, 227, 241–2).

[86] See (8:396fn), (9:82), (R2583, 16:427), (R2600, 16:435), (R2602, 16:436), (20:299), and (24:143–4, 194, 427, 433–6, 555, 742, 883).

something probable' (24:825). On Kant's account, then, we are rationally permitted to hold the opinion that p even if we know that the probability of $\neg p$ is close to but less than 0.5, and therefore that $\neg p$ is almost as likely as p.

Indeed, Kant might even allow for some (rational) opinions that are less than 0.5 probable. To see why, we need to look at a 'special kind of . . . opinion', namely, hypothesis (24:220). A hypothesis is defined as 'a proposition that one assumes to explain certain phenomena' (29:918). Kant specifies that a given phenomenon can be explained by several hypotheses 'for there may be several causes of one and the same effect', adding that, to be rational, we should choose the hypothesis that is 'most probable' (29:104). But the most probable hypothesis needn't be more probable than not, as illustrated by:[87]

> **Murder**. Sherlock investigates a murder with five suspects: Ann, Ben, Chris, Dan, and Eric. Sherlock knows that all but Ann are family members known to be on great terms with the victim. Ann, however, has a history of verbally aggressive interactions with the victim. The probabilities for each suspect being the murderer are Pr(Ann) = 0.48 and Pr(Ben) = Pr(Chris) = Pr(Dan) = Pr(Eric) = 0.13. Pending further evidence, Sherlock rationally hypothesizes, and so holds the opinion, that Ann committed the murder.

Would Kant agree that it is irrational to be convinced that p or certain that p if one knows that: while p is more likely than ¬p, ¬p is almost as likely as p (T7)? Answer: Yes. Remember that according to Kant both logical certainty and conviction that p require robust evidence in the form of sufficient objective grounds for p. On an infallibilist reading,[88] these grounds must entail p and, thus, guarantee that p has probability 1. This infalliblist reading is well supported. As noted before, Kant defines all degrees of probability as degrees of certainty, implying that certain assent has probability 1. In fact, Kant states more generally that 'the sufficient ground is the one whose opposite cannot possibly be thought and represented to be true' (24:145). This statement should apply to both logical certainty and conviction, which both rest on such sufficient objective grounds.[89]

For reasons that we cannot discuss here, not all interpreters agree with this infallibilist reading of sufficient objective grounds. Most notably, Chignell (2007a, 2007b, 2021) has advanced a fallibilist reading on which sufficient objective grounds can come with a probability shy of 1 and needn't entail the

[87] On improbable opinion in Kant, see also Chignell (2007a:327,2007b:44,2021:119). See footnote 16.

[88] See, for example, Pasternack (2014), Willaschek and Watkins (2020:3207), and Kern (2021:120).

[89] As noted in footnote 79, Kant's definition of probability (as ratio of the objective ground we have to the sufficient objective ground) may already entail that assent from sufficient objective grounds must have a probability of 1. However, see Chignell (2007b:40) for an alternative reading.

truth of an assent.[90] But even on this fallibilist reading, sufficient objective grounds must render an assent 'probable to a degree that is comfortably more than .5' (Chignell 2007b:43), in which case p is much more likely than $\neg p$. So on both infallibilist and fallibilist readings of Kant, subjective conviction and subjective certainty must be normatively strong. Therefore, Kant must be read as accepting T7.

In this section we have made the case that Kant's theory of assent deserves the label 'Kantian', in our sense of the term. After all, Kant's account shares many core features of the Kantian Threshold View. Most notably, Kant gives prominence to (subjective) opinion, conviction, and certainty, which constitutively involve doxastic states of assent that are ordered by their doxastic strength. Moreover, Kant appears to have the resources to specify the strength of these doxastic states in terms of degrees of conviction. So even if Kant would have self-identified as a Lockean, his account strikes us as distinctly Kantian.

7.2 Belief in Kant

Having specified Kant's account of opinion, conviction, and certainty, we now turn to the notion of belief. While our present-day notion of belief shouldn't be identified with Kant's notion of *Glaube* (which can be translated as capital-B 'Belief' or 'faith'), we can still ask: What outright doxastic attitude in Kant best aligns with what contemporary anglo-analytic philosophers call 'belief'? Specifically, would Kant have preferred B=T, or B=C, or B=A from Section 4.2? We argue that Kant would likely have endorsed B=A because his concept of assent (*Fürwahrhalten*) comes closest to belief.

There are two positive reasons for this identity. First, note that in English – or at least the English idiolect of anglophone analytic philosophers – thinking, conviction, and certainty all entail believing. Since Kant held that assent is the genus of which (subjective) opinion, conviction, and certainty are species (A822–9/B850–7), he must have thought that the same conditionals also hold for assent. That is, opinion (/thinking), conviction, and certainty all entail assent (see conditionals below). This parallel suggests a *structural* similarity between anglo-analytic uses of 'belief' and Kant's use of '*Fürwahrhalten*':

T→B: If S thinks that p, then S believes that p.
O(=T)→A: If it is S's opinion that p (/S thinks that p), then S assents to p.
Wenn es S' Meinung ist, dass p, dann hält S p für wahr.

[90] For other fallibilist readings of Kant, see Gava (2016), Cohen (2021:694), and Hebbeler (2021:736).

Con→B: If *S* is convinced that *p*, then *S* believes that *p*.
Con→A: If *S* is convinced that *p*, then *S* assents to *p*.
Wenn S (davon) überzeugt ist, dass p, dann hält S p für wahr.

Cert→B: If *S* is certain that *p*, then *S* believes that *p*.
Cert→A: If *S* is certain that *p*, then *S* assents to *p*.
Wenn S (sich) gewiss ist, dass p, dann hält S p für wahr.

Second, there is also a *semantic* similarity between 'belief' and 'assent'/ '*Fürwahrhalten*'. For Kant, 'assenting to *p*' simply means 'holding *p* as true'. But what could it be to hold *p* as true in the absence of a disposition to rely on *p*? In fact, as briefly noted earlier, Kant thinks that we can measure the doxastic strength of assent by how much we are willing to bet on the assent being true. In the case of a doxastically weak assent, we might bet only 'one ducat' ('*Dukaten*'); however, if the assent is stronger, we might bet ten ducats (A824/B853). And if the assent reaches a maximum strength, then we gain psychological or subjective certainty and we would, Kant says, 'bet the happiness of the entire life' (A825/B853).

This link between assenting and betting suggests that Kant thinks of degrees of assent in terms of the strength of a disposition to rely on a proposition. For Kant, the disposition to bet on an assent being true seems to indicate not a feeling or phenomenal conviction, but at least a disposition to act on various propositions. It seems very plausible to us that this idea is just a matter of being disposed to rely on *p* in various ways. For what else could it mean to hold *p* as true without being willing to rely on *p* in at least some ways, such as asserting, acting, or deliberating? This fits well with Minimal Nature and DoC.[91] So *holding p as true* and *relying on p* – which is connected to the contemporary anglo-analytic notion of 'belief' – seem to be getting at the same idea.

This semantic link receives additional support from Kant's account of suspension. Recall that our dispositional analysis of belief allowed for believing suspension, that is, cases in which we believe that *p* and at the same time suspend belief that *p*. Curiously, Kant seems to suggest something similar for assent, stating that opinion is compatible with suspension: 'In opinion, [we are] in suspension' (R2463, 16:381).[92] Such passages motivate the thought that, for Kant, assent is compatible with suspension, and that assent has a similar dispositional nature to

[91] Though Kant would not have articulated these principles using possible worlds semantics.

[92] See also (9:66–7), (R2450, 16:374), (R2459, 16:378–9), and (R2511, 16:399). Note also that opinion in the cited passage means *mere* opinion, which makes sense since, as suggested in Section 6.3, we cannot have believing suspension in cases of (absolute) subjective certainty. Kant's account of suspension invokes sophisticated distinctions between different kinds of judgement, but these are distinctions we cannot discuss here.

belief; after all, it is the dispositional nature of belief that made believing suspension possible.[93]

Although B=A has much going for it, Chignell raises two objections. The first objection says that Kant's notion of assent can be weaker than our notion of belief. On Chignell's (2007b) reading, assent includes 'hunches, working assumptions, scientific hypotheses, and other weakly-held opinions' (37; emphasis omitted), some of which Chignell wouldn't call beliefs. In response to this objection, recall that opinion can involve a low degree of conviction, as we saw in Track Race and Diagnosis. Of course, Chignell would insist that we wouldn't categorize all weakly held opinions as beliefs, for example, hunches seem too weak. But against this notice that 'It's my hunch that *p*' and 'I think that *p*'/'I'm at least somewhat convinced that *p*' in contexts like Track Race, Diagnosis, and even Murder, seem to refer to the same doxastic state.

But there is, perhaps, more to be said for Chignell's position. After all, *if* no belief is weaker than the ones in Track Race and Diagnosis, and *if* Kant accepts assent as weak as the one in Murder, then some types of assent would really be weaker than what we would call belief. However, those are two controversial 'ifs'. Denying the first 'if', some epistemologists have argued that the lower bound of thinking can be pushed down much closer to the zero-degree endpoint than what is suggested by Track Race and Diagnosis (Holguín 2022). Denying the second 'if', some interpreters have insisted that Kant could not have accepted Murder because opinion requires a probability of above 0.5 (Pasternack 2014). Either move would preserve our position.

Chignell's second objection says that assent, in Kant's sense, can stand under direct voluntary control, whereas belief, in our sense, can't (Chignell 2007a:341–4,2007b:56). We agree with Chignell that Kant endorses a direct doxastic voluntarism for some species of assent. This not only goes for Belief or faith (see Section 2.1), but also for opinion, which Chignell (2007b:38) claims is at least 'sometimes voluntary'. We would go even further. There is strong textual evidence to think that opinion, as mere opinion, always falls under our direct voluntary control. Because (i) all 'opinion is a problematic . . . judgement'

[93] There are, however, some features of Kant's account of suspension that distinguish it from our account of believing suspension. For one thing, Kant thinks that, in the case of opinion, we don't suspend opinion but prejudice (R2523, 16:404), which is the 'propensity towards persuasion' (24:547). Indeed, opinion is the result of this suspension. Moreover, Kant thinks that *every* opinion requires such a suspension of prejudice or persuasion (cf. the passages from footnote 92). And finally, opinion, as suspension of prejudice or persuasion, is not to be understood as a self-masking of the disposition to rely on *p* in every way, but only in some ways. For example, if *S* has the opinion that *p*, *S* must not assert that *p* (A821–2/B849–50). But *S* can (and should) appeal to *p* in the quest for further evidence (R2512, 16:399).

(9:66), and (ii) all problematic judgements allow for 'free choice' and are therefore 'merely voluntary [*willkürliche*] assumption[s]' (A75/B101).[94]

However, this doxastic voluntarism is not clearly inconsistent with the dispositional analysis of belief. After all, we can choose to rely on *p*. If our choice is sufficiently efficacious we might rely on *p* in a proportion of worlds large enough to count as thinking that *p*. At the very least, further argument is needed to show that a doxastic state as dispositionally weak as thinking is never under one's direct voluntary control. This turns, we suspect, on delicate matters concerning how the relevant worlds are specified. We cannot explore that here.

Silva noted in conversation that Kant's taxonomy of doxastic assent also affords us the resources to resist Hawthornes et al.'s (2016) identification of believing and thinking, that is, B=T, for the primary evidence for B=T is the apparent logical equivalence of '*S* believes that *p*' and '*S* thinks that *p*' (B↔T). But we can get B↔T without B=T from: (i) B=A, (ii) the Kantian Threshold View, and (iii) any view on which belief/assent is a general state with thinking/opinion, conviction, and certainty as its only outright instances.[95] For if (iii) holds, then thinking/opinion entails belief/assent. And (ii), the Kantian Threshold View, has it that thinking/opinion is entailed by conviction and by certainty. Since the only way to realize the general state of *belief/assent* is by realizing one of its more specific instances, and since all of its outright instances entail thinking, it follows that believing entails thinking. So we get B↔T. But we do not get B=T because the general state is not to be identified with its more specific instances.

In our view, then, B=A is certainly no less well supported than B=C and B=T. Additionally, B=A seems to be at least slightly more favoured by the evidence, that is, the evidence favours the idea that 'belief' as used in anglo-analytic philosophy is co-referential with the term '*Fürwahrhalten*' as used by Kant. While the connection between belief and assent has already been noted by Crane (2013), Schwitzgebel (2023), and others, we hope to have added robust Kantian support for the view.

[94] On the voluntary profile of opinion see (R2449, 16:372–3), (R2462, 16:381), and (R2463, 16:381), as well as Benzenberg (forthcoming). For an involuntarist reading of Kant, see Cohen (2021).

[95] (iii) follows from a genus-species claim about the relation between assent and thinking, conviction, and certainty. But the genus-species claim is open to an objection because distinct species of a genus are usually mutually exclusive. But certainty, conviction, and thinking are not mutually exclusive on the Kantian Threshold View. But one may alternatively consider belief/assent as a determinable, with specific degrees of conviction as an ordered set of determinants. Thinking, conviction, and certainty would, on this model, just be increasingly inclusive sets of mutually exclusive, determinate degrees of conviction. For an analogy, consider *being red* versus its determinates: *being crimson, being blood orange, being coral red, being rust red,* and so on. Next: think of classifying the determinates of red in terms of how close they come to orange (not at all orange, at least somewhat orange, almost orange). This is an example of a generality relation closer to what was proposed in Section 3 with the Kantian Threshold View.

References

Aimar, Simona (2019). Disposition Ascriptions. *Philosophical Studies* 176 (7):1667–1692.

Ashwell, Lauren (2010). Superficial Dispositionalism. *Australasian Journal of Philosophy* 88 (4):1–19.

Atkins, Philip (2017). A Russellian Account of Suspended Judgment. *Synthese* 194:3021–3046.

Beddor, Bob (2020). New Work For Certainty. *Philosophers' Imprint* 20 (8):1–25.

Beddor, Bob & Pavese, Carlotta (2020). Modal Virtue Epistemology. *Philosophy and Phenomenological Research* 101 (1):61–79.

Benzenberg, Christopher (forthcoming). Room for Responsibility: Kant on Direct Doxastic Voluntarism. *Inquiry.*

Borgoni, Cristina, Kindermann, Dirk, & Onofri, Andrea (2021). *The Fragmented Mind.* Oxford University Press.

Bricker, Adam Michael (2022). I Hear You Feel Confident. *Philosophical Quarterly* 73 (1):24–43.

Buchak, Lara (2014). Belief, Credence, and Norms. *Philosophical Studies* 169 (2):1–27.

Chalmers, David (1996). *The Conscious Mind.* Oxford University Press.

Chignell, Andrew (2007a). Belief in Kant. *Philosophical Review* 116 (3):323–360.

Chignell, Andrew (2007b). Kant's Concepts of Justification. *Noûs* 41 (1):33–63.

Chignell, Andrew (2021). Kantian Fallibilism: Knowledge, Certainty, Doubt. *Midwest Studies in Philosophy* 45:99–128.

Choi, Sungho (2013). Can Opposing Dispositions Be Co-instantiated? *Erkenntnis* 78 (1):161–182.

Choi, Sungho (2017). Against Intrinsic Interferers: A Critique of Kittle. *Philosophical Quarterly* 67 (269):845–854.

Christensen, David (2007). Epistemology of Disagreement: The Good News. *Philosophical Review* 116:187–218.

Clarke, Randolph (2010). Opposing Powers. *Philosophical Studies* 149 (2): 153–160.

Clarke, Roger (2013). Belief Is Credence One (in Context). *Philosophers' Imprint* 13 (11):1–18.

Clarke, Roger & Staffel, Julia (2023). Are Credences Different From Beliefs? In Blake Roeber, Matthias Steup, John Turri, & Ernest Sosa (eds.), *Contemporary Debates in Epistemology*, 3rd edition. Wiley Blackwell, 229–252.

Cohen, Alix (2021). Kant on Epistemic Autonomy. In C. Serck-Hanssen & B. Himmelmann (eds.), *The Court of Reason: Proceedings of the 13th International Kant Congress*. De Gruyter, 687–696.

Crane, Tim (2013). Unconscious Belief and Conscious Thought. In Uriah Kriegel (ed.), *Phenomenal Intentionality*. Oxford University Press, 156–173.

Dorst, Kevin (2019). Lockeans Maximize Expected Accuracy. *Mind* 128 (509):175–211.

Eriksson, Lina & Hájek, Alan (2007). What Are Degrees of Belief? *Studia Logica* 86 (2):185–215.

Everett, Anthony (2009). Intrinsic Finks, Masks, and Mimics. *Erkenntnis* 71 (2):191–203.

Field, Hartry (1978). Mental Representation. *Erkenntnis* 13:9–61.

Fodor, Jerry (1990). *A Theory of Content and Other Essays*. MIT Press.

Foley, Richard (1992). The Epistemology of Belief and the Epistemology of Degrees of Belief. *American Philosophical Quarterly* 29 (2):111–124.

Foley, Richard (1993). *Working Without a Net: A Study of Egocentric Epistemology*. Oxford University Press.

Frankish, Keith (2009). Partial Belief and Flat-out Belief. In Franz Huber & Christoph Schmidt-Petri (eds.), *Degrees of Belief*. Springer, 75–93.

Friedman, Jane (2017). Why Suspend Judging? *Noûs* 51 (2):302–326.

Friedman, Jane (2019). Inquiry and Belief. *Noûs* 53 (2):296–315.

Friend, Toby & Kimpton-Nye, Samuel (2023). *Dispositions and Powers*. Cambridge University Press.

Gava, Gabriele (2016). The Fallibilism of Kant's Architectonic. In G. Gava & R. Stern (eds.), *Pragmatism, Kant, and Transcendental Philosophy*. Routledge, 46–66.

Gava, Gabriele (2019). Kant and Crucius on Belief and Practical Justification. *Kantian Review* 24 (1):53–71.

Gava, Gabriele (2024). Kant on Conviction and Persuasion. In Luigi Filieri & Sofie Møller (eds.), *Kant on Freedom and Human Nature*. Routledge, 135–150.

Goodman, Jeremy (2023). The Myth of Full Belief. *Philosophical Perspectives* 37 (1):164–171. https://doi.org/10.1111/phpe.12185.

Goodman, Jeremy & Holguín, Ben (2023). Thinking and Being Sure. *Philosophy and Phenomenological Research* 106 (3):634–654.

Greco, Daniel (2015). How I Learned to Stop Worrying and Love Probability 1. *Philosophical Perspectives* 29 (1):179–201.

Greco, Daniel (2023). *Idealization in Epistemology*. Oxford University Press.

Greco, John (2010). *Achieving Knowledge: A Virtue-Theoretic Account of Epistemic Normativity*. Cambridge University Press.

Handfield, Toby (2008). Unfinkable Dispositions. *Synthese* 160 (2):297–308.

Hannon, Michael (2019). *What's the Point of Knowledge? A Function-First Epistemology*. Oxford University Press.

Harman, Gilbert (1986). *Change in View: Principles of Reasoning*. MIT Press.

Hawthorne, John, Rothschild, Daniel, & Spectre, Levi (2016). Belief is Weak. *Philosophical Studies* 173 (5):1393–1404.

Hebbeler, James (2021). Reason, Reflection, and Reliabilism: Kant and the Grounds of Rational and Empirical Knowledge. In C. Serck-Hanssen & B. Himmelmann (eds.), *The Court of Reason: Proceedings of the 13th International Kant Congress*. De Gruyter, 735–742.

Heil, Roman (2021). Knowledge and Rational Action. *Why What We Know Matters for the Rationality of What We Do*. Unpublished Doctoral Dissertation. University of Hamburg.

Holguín, Ben (2022). Thinking, Guessing, and Believing. *Philosophers' Imprint* 22 (1):1–34.

Hyman, John (2017). Knowledge and Belief. *Aristotelian Society Supplementary* 91:267–288.

Insole, Christopher J. (2019). Free Belief: The Medieval Heritage in Kant's Moral Faith. *Journal of the History of Philosophy* 57 (3):501–528.

Jackson, Elizabeth (2020a). Belief, Credence, and Evidence. *Synthese* 197 (11):5073–5092.

Jackson, Elizabeth (2020b). The Relationship Between Belief and Credence. *Philosophy Compass* 15 (6):1–13.

Johnston, Mark (1992). How to Speak of the Colors. *Philosophical Studies* 68 (3):221–263.

Kant, Immanuel (1900). *Kants Gesammelte Schriften. Königlich-Preußische Akademie* der Wissenschaften (ed.). De Gruyter.

Kant, Immanuel (1998). *Kritik der reinen Vernunft*. Jens Timmermann (ed.). Felix Meiner Verlag.

Kelly, Thomas (2005). The Epistemic Significance of Disagreement. In T. Gendler & J. Hawthorne (eds.), *Oxford Studies in Epistemology*: Volume 1. Oxford University Press, 7–196.

Kennedy, Christopher (2007). Vagueness and Grammar: The Semantics of Relative and Absolute Gradable Adjectives. *Linguistics and Philosophy* 30 (1):1–45.

Kern, Andrea (2021). Kant on Doubt and Error. *Midwest Studies in Philosophy* 45:129–154.

Kittle, Simon (2015). Powers Opposed and Intrinsic Finks. *Philosophical Quarterly* 65 (260):372–380.

Krifka, Manfred (2002). Be Brief and Vague! And How Bidirectional Optimality Theory Allows for Verbosity and Precision. In D. Restle &

D. Zaefferer (eds.), *Sounds and Systems, Studies in Structure and Change: A Festschrift for Theo Vennemann*. Mouton de Gruyter, 439–458.

Krifka, Manfred (2007). Approximate Interpretations of Number Words: A Case of Strategic Communication. In G. Bouma, I. Kramer, & J. Zwarts (eds.), *Cognitive Foundations of Interpretation*. Koninklijke Nederlandse Akademie van Wetenschapen, 111–126.

Lakoff, George (1973). Hedges: A Study in Meaning Criteria and the Logic of Fuzzy Concepts. *Journal of Philosophical Logic* 2:458–508.

Leitgeb, Hannes (2017). *The Stability of Belief.* Oxford University Press.

Lewis, David (1979). Scorekeeping in a Language Game. *Journal of Philosophical Logic* 8 (3):339–359.

Locke, John (1975). *An Essay Concerning Human Understanding*. Peter H. Nidditch (ed.). Clarendon Press.

Lord, Errol (2020). Suspension of Judgment, Rationality's Competition, and the Reach of the Epistemic. In S. Schmidt & G. Ernst (eds.), *The Ethics of Belief and Beyond*. Routledge, 126–145.

Lyons, Jack C. (2009). *Perception and Basic Beliefs: Zombies, Modules and the Problem of the External World*. Jack Lyons (ed.). Oxford University Press.

Manley, David & Wasserman, Ryan (2007). A Gradable Approach to Dispositions. *Philosophical Quarterly* 57 (226):68–75.

Manley, David & Wasserman, Ryan (2008). On Linking Dispositions and Conditionals. *Mind* 117 (465):59–84.

Manley, David & Wasserman, Ryan (2011). Dispositions, Conditionals, and Counterexamples. *Mind* 120 (480):1191–1227.

McGrath, Matthew (2021a). Being Neutral: Agnosticism, Inquiry and the Suspension of Judgment. *Noûs* 55 (2):463–484.

McGrath, Matthew (2021b). Epistemic Norms for Waiting. *Philosophical Topics* 49 (2):173–201.

Meier, Georg F. (1752). *Auszug aus der Vernunftlehre*. Johann Justinus Gebauer.

Miller, Christian (2014). *Character and Moral Psychology*. Oxford University Press.

Miracchi, Lisa (2019). When Evidence Isn't Enough: Suspension, Evidentialism, and Knowledge-First Virtue Epistemology. *Episteme* 16 (4):413–437.

Moon, Andrew (2018). The Nature of Doubt and a New Puzzle about Belief, Doubt, and Confidence. *Synthese* 195 (4):1827–1848.

Moon, Andrew & Jackson, Elizabeth (2020). Credence: A Belief-First Approach. *Canadian Journal of Philosophy* 50 (5):652–669.

Pasternack, Lawrence (2011). The Development and Scope of Kantian Belief: The Highest-Good, The Practical Postulates, and the Fact of Reason. *Kant-Studien* 102 (3):290–315.

Pasternack, Lawrence (2014). Kant on Opinion: Assent, Hypothesis, and the Norms of General Applied Logic. *Kant-Studien* 105 (1):41–82.

Pinkal, Manfred (1995). *Logic and Lexicon*. Kluwer.

Raleigh, Thomas (2021). Suspending is Believing. *Synthese* 198:2449–2474

Ross, Jacob & Schroeder, Mark (2014). Belief, Credence, and Pragmatic Encroachment. *Philosophy and Phenomenological Research* 88 (2):259–288.

Rothschild, Daniel (2020). What It Takes to Believe. *Philosophical Studies* 177 (5):1345–1362.

Rotstein, Carmen & Winter, Yoad (2004). Total Adjectives vs. Partial Adjectives: Scale Structure and Higher-Order Modifiers. *Natural Language Semantics* 12 (3):259–288.

Sadock, Jerrold (1977). Truth and Approximations. In K. Whistler Jr., R.D. Van Valin, C. Chiarello, et al. (eds.), *Proceedings of the Third Annual Meeting of the Berkeley Linguistics Society*. Berkeley Linguistics Society.

Sauerland, Uli & Stateva, Penka (2007). Scalar vs. Epistemic Vagueness: Evidence from Approximators. In T. Friedman and M. Gibson (eds.), *Proceedings of the 17th Semantics and Linguistic Theory Conference*. CLC Publishing, 228–245.

Schroeder, Mark (2015). *Knowledge Is Belief for Sufficient (Objective and Subjective) Reason*. Oxford Studies in Epistemology 5, 226–251.

Schulz, Moritz (2021a). Strong Knowledge, Weak Belief? *Synthese* 199 (3–4):8741–8753.

Schulz, Moritz (2021b). Practical Reasoning and Degrees of Outright Belief. *Synthese* 199 (3–4):8069–8090.

Schwitzgebel, Eric (2002). A Phenomenal, Dispositional Account of Belief. *Noûs* 36 (2):249–275.

Schwitzgebel, Eric (2023). Belief. In Edward N. Zalta & Uri Nodelman (eds.), The Stanford Encyclopedia of Philosophy (Winter 2023 Edition), https://plato.stanford.edu/archives/win2023/entries/belief/.

Silva, Paul (2016). How Doxastic Justification Helps Us Solve the Puzzle of Misleading Higher-Order Evidence. *Pacific Philosophical Quarterly* 98 (S1):308–328.

Silva, Paul (2023a). Merely Statistical Evidence: When and Why It Justifies Belief. *Philosophical Studies* 180 (9):2639–2664.

Silva, Paul (2023b). *Awareness and the Substructure of Knowledge*. Oxford University Press.

Skyrms, Brian (2011). Resiliency, Propensities, and Causal Necessity. In Antony Eagle (ed.), *Philosophy of Probability: Contemporary Readings*. Routledge.

Smith, Martin (2016). *Between Probability and Certainty: What Justifies Belief.* Oxford University Press.

Smithies, Declan (2023). Belief as a Feeling of Conviction. In Eric Schwitzgebel & Jonathan Jong (eds.), *The Nature of Belief.* Oxford University Press.

Sosa, Ernest (2015). *Judgment and Agency.* Oxford University Press.

Sosa, Ernest (2019). Suspension as Spandrel. *Episteme* 16(4):357–368.

Staffel, Julia (2016). Beliefs, Buses and Lotteries: Why Rational Belief Can't Be Stably High Credence. *Philosophical Studies* 173 (7):1721–1734.

Staffel, Julia (2019). Credences and Suspended Judgments as Transitional Attitudes. *Philosophical Issues* 29(1):281–294.

Stalnaker, Robert C. (1984). *Inquiry.* Cambridge University Press.

Stevenson, Leslie (2003). Opinion, Belief or Faith, and Knowledge. *Kantian Review* 7:72–101.

Sturgeon, Scott (2010). Confidence and Coarse-Grained Attitudes. In T. Gendler & J. Hawthorne (eds.), *Oxford Studies in Epistemology:* Volume 3. Oxford University Press, 3–126.

Sylvan, Kurt (2015). What Apparent Reasons Appear to Be. *Philosophical Studies* 172 (3):587–606.

Titelbaum, Michael (2015). Rationality's Fixed Point (Or: In Defense of Right Reason). In J. Hawthorne & T. Gendler (eds.), *Oxford Studies in Epistemology:* Volume 5. Oxford University Press, 253–294.

Turri, John (2015). Unreliable Knowledge. *Philosophy and Phenomenological Research* 90 (3):529–545.

Turri, John (2016). A New Paradigm for Epistemology From Reliabilism to Abilism. *Ergo: An Open Access Journal of Philosophy* 3:189–231.

Unger, Peter K. (1975). *Ignorance*. Oxford University Press.

Vetter, Barbara (2015). *Potentiality: From Dispositions to Modality.* Oxford University Press.

Wagner, Verena (2022). Agnosticism As Settled Indecision. *Philosophical Studies* 179 (2):671–697.

Wedgwood, Ralph (2002). The Aim of Belief. *Philosophical Perspectives* 16:267–297.

Wedgwood, Ralph (2023). *Rationality and Belief.* Oxford University Press.

Weisberg, Jonathan (2020). Belief in Psyontology. *Philosophers' Imprint* 20 (11):1–27.

White, Roger (2005). Epistemic Permissiveness. *Philosophical Perspectives* 19 (1):445–459.

Willaschek, Marcus (2010): The Primacy of Practical Reason and the Idea of a Practical Postulate. In Andrews Reath & Jens Timmermann (eds.), *Kant's Critique of Practical Reason, A Critical Guide*. Cambridge University Press, 168–196.

Willaschek, Marcus & Watkins, Eric (2020). Kant on Cognition and Knowledge. *Synthese* 197 (8):3195–3213.

Williamson, Timothy (2000). *Knowledge and Its Limits*. Oxford University Press.

Zimmerman, Aaron (2018). *Belief: A Pragmatic Picture*. Oxford University Press.

Zinke, Alexandra (2021). Rational Suspension. *Theoria* 87 (5):1050–1066.

Acknowledgements

This Element would not be what it is without the comments and reactions to drafts of this material provided by Christopher Benzenberg, Marvin Backes, Lena Ghareh Baghery, Aliosha Barranco Lopez, John Bengson, Sven Bernecker, Jochen Briesen, Andrew Chignell, Kenny Easwaran, Jane Friedman, Martin Grajner, Daniel Greco, Thomas Grundman, Roman Heil, Stephen Hetherington, Hatice Kaya, Carline Klijnman, Uriah Kriegel, Daniel Lassiter, Jack Lyons, Farid Masrour, Matthew McGrath, Luis Rosa, Joshua Schechter, Eva Schmidt, Moritz Schulz, Wes Siscoe, Julia Staffel, Jesse Steinberg, Michael Titelbaum, Verena Wagner, Brian Weatherson, Simon Wimmer, Alexandra Zinke, and the Cambridge referees. Thank you all!

For my German colleagues, who warmly welcomed me into their rich intellectual community.

Cambridge Elements

Epistemology

Stephen Hetherington
University of New South Wales, Sydney

Stephen Hetherington is Professor Emeritus of Philosophy at the University of New South Wales, Sydney. He is the author of numerous books, including *Knowledge and the Gettier Problem* (Cambridge University Press, 2016), and *What Is Epistemology?* (Polity, 2019), and is the editor of several others, including *Knowledge in Contemporary Epistemology* (with Markos Valaris: Bloomsbury, 2019), and *What the Ancients Offer to Contemporary Epistemology* (with Nicholas D. Smith: Routledge, 2020). He was the Editor-in-Chief of the Australasian Journal of Philosophy from 2013 until 2022.

About the Series

This Elements series seeks to cover all aspects of a rapidly evolving field, including emerging and evolving topics such as: fallibilism; knowing how; self-knowledge; knowledge of morality; knowledge and injustice; formal epistemology; knowledge and religion; scientific knowledge; collective epistemology; applied epistemology; virtue epistemology; wisdom. The series demonstrates the liveliness and diversity of the field, while also pointing to new areas of investigation.

Cambridge Elements

Epistemology

Elements in the Series

The A Priori *Without Magic*
Jared Warren

Defining Knowledge: Method and Metaphysics
Stephen Hetherington

Wisdom: A Skill Theory
Cheng-hung Tsai

Higher-Order Evidence and Calibrationism
Ru Ye

The Nature and Normativity of Defeat
Christoph Kelp

Stratified Virtue Epistemology: A Defence
J. Adam Carter

Philosophy, Bullshit, and Peer Review
Neil Levy

The Skeptic and the Veridicalist: On the Difference Between Knowing What There Is and Knowing What Things Are
Yuval Avnur

Transcendental Epistemology
Tony Cheng

Knowledge and God
Matthew A. Benton

Disagreement
Diego E. Machuca

On Believing and Being Convinced
Paul Silva Jr

A full series listing is available at: www.cambridge.org/EEPI

For EU product safety concerns, contact us at Calle de José Abascal, 56–1°, 28003 Madrid, Spain or eugpsr@cambridge.org.

www.ingramcontent.com/pod-product-compliance
Ingram Content Group UK Ltd.
Pitfield, Milton Keynes, MK11 3LW, UK
UKHW022144080726
473066UK00010B/749

* 9 7 8 1 0 0 9 5 2 4 1 5 5 *